IRRESISTIBLE LOVE

IRRESISTIBLE LOVE

A JOURNEY TO THE HEART OF JESUS

JOE WHITE

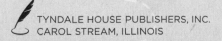

TYNDALE HOUSE PUBLISHERS, INC.
CAROL STREAM, ILLINOIS

FOCUS ON THE FAMILY®

To Debbie-Jo

My bride, my hero, my best friend.

As with Jesus, your love has been irresistible for more than 50 years.

How blessed can a man get!

CONTENTS

INTRODUCTION

"Whatever you've known of Jesus before . . ."

THIS BOOK IS NOT the last word on Jesus, nor is it an attempt to be the most informative, compelling, or insightful book about the Man Major Ian Thomas referred to as "Christ, the Astonishing Preacher," and of whom Albert Einstein remarked, "I am a Jew, but I am enthralled by the luminous figure of the Nazarene."

This book is, however, the story of the Man of the cross as He has revealed Himself to me over my 67-year journey to His heart through life's ever-educating laboratory, through His inspired Word, and through countless encounters with both young and old, illustrious and downtrodden, learned and uneducated, optimistic and hopeless.

This book is an old and broken author's attempt to open a window into what I believe is a lifetime's greatest quest: to know "the breadth and length and height and depth" and to know the irresistible love of God not casually, not superficially, not religiously or merely cognitively, but to begin to know Him as, indeed, we have been fully known.

As I handwrite this introduction from my blue leather seat aboard my flight to San Antonio to undergo open-heart surgery, I can promise one thing: This book will be raw and authentic; there will be no far-fetched theories, no ghost-writer, and no made-up stories. Am I fearful of the surgery and the weeks of recovery? My shaky handwriting today would say *yes*. But, as I've gone under the knife so many times before, I believe wholeheartedly every word in this book and in the "Author and Perfecter of our faith" of whom this book is written.

Just as my heart surgeon will go deep into my beleaguered coronary system, where the manufacturer's warranty has outlived the manufacturer's guarantee, I hope to dig deeply and honestly into the gold mine of faith together with you.

To a football coach, "going deep" means to send a receiver far down the gridiron for a long bomb from the quarterback, hoping for a spectacular pass play. To a scuba diver, "going deep" means to explore marvelous places on a hidden coral reef that few have set their gaze upon. To a spelunker, "going deep" means to crawl far into unexplored crystal caverns where the stalactites, stalagmites, and gypsum crystals are unharmed and virgin pure.

To a Christian counselor, "going deep" means having the privilege to listen patiently to someone who's hurting and to coexperience the healing work of an empathetic Savior who "pardons all your iniquities, who heals all your diseases, who redeems your life from the pit, who crowns you with loving-kindness and compassion" (Psalm 103:3-4).

But to an author who has spent four decades preparing to write a book that could perhaps take a curious hitchhiker on a journey of fulfilling intimacy, "going deep" means to know richly the One of whom David prophesied as Mark 11:9 says, "Hosanna! Blessed is He who comes in the name of the Lord."

He's the One whom Isaiah would refer to as "Wonderful

Counselor, Mighty God, Eternal Father, Prince of Peace" (Isaiah 9:6).

Yes, He's the One whose works and observances permeate the libraries of the world, far excelling any other figure in human history. He is the most quoted teacher who ever instructed and the most widely admired figure who ever lived.

William Shakespeare said that Jesus was his "Saviour, my Hope, my Creator. Apart from His mercy I have no hope for eternal life."[1]

Charles Dickens said, "The New Testament is the very best book that ever was or ever will be known in the world."[2]

John Grisham said, "Accepting Jesus Christ was the most important event in my life."[3]

Johann Sebastian Bach, considered in music as the "Master of masters," said, "Jesus is my joy."[4]

Blaise Pascal, father of the science of hydrostatics and differential calculus, said Jesus is the true "God of men. Without Jesus there is only sin, misery, darkness, death, and despair."[5]

President Abraham Lincoln said His Word was "the best gift God has given to man."[6]

Mother Teresa said, "I serve because I love Jesus."[7]

At a post-game appearance with reporters on December 4, 2015, LeBron James said, "There's only one guy ever in the world that everything will be all right when He comes back, and that's Jesus Christ."[8]

And most importantly, Jesus is the One of whom God said, "This is My beloved Son, in whom I am well-pleased" (Matthew 3:17).

Finally, to me, this book is meant to awaken your fascination with the One who loves you so much that He gave His life as a ransom for your soul.

PART ONE

FINDING GOD'S IRRESISTIBLE LOVE

1

WHO'S YOUR JESUS?

THE "AMERICAN JESUS" has blue eyes, fair skin, and wavy, light-brown hair discreetly highlighted with sandy blond streaks. His hands are soft and tender, and His beautiful scarlet and purple robes have just been returned from the dry cleaner. He is warm, cuddly, and always plays it safe. Traveling with Him is like traveling with a sweet, quiet, old grandpa who's a friend to everybody. You meet Him in church on Sunday morning between 10:30 and noon, late enough to ensure a good night's rest on Saturday but not too late to miss the opening kickoff between the Cowboys and the Redskins. During church, beautiful love songs are sung to Him, and you're left feeling cozy and "worshipful." The lights and sounds create the perfect ambience, along with the mastered audiovisual effects projecting pleasant color palettes on the giant screens before you.

It all feels so . . . He seems so . . . He makes life feel so . . . so predictable, so safe, so comfortable.

If He were a pristine coral reef, you could observe Him by merely placing a dive mask over your face and a snorkel in your mouth. You could smoothly skim the surface of the tranquil, blue water below with no risk of fright from a green eel waiting motionless between two coral-laden rocks for his next unfortunate capture. Nor would you have to worry about a spiny prick on your skin from a barnacle waving its gypsum-like arms in an attempt to woo a small, helpless nutrient into its grasp.

This is the American Jesus. To snorkel safely above Him brings promise of financial prosperity and pain-free living.

Perhaps you've met Him. Perhaps you've admired Him. Perhaps you've "accepted Him" as "Savior" or even "Lord." Perhaps you've watched Him on many Sunday mornings from the comfort of your church pew or auditorium-style chair.

For our convenience, we can even snorkel above Him from the cozy couch in our climate-controlled living room as He parades before us on our 54-inch flat-screen TV when it's a little too damp and chilly to go outside or when the golf foursome was forced to take an 11:00 a.m. tee time.

American Jesus. He's pictured on billboards and T-shirts throughout the land. He hangs delicately on a smooth, golden cross awaiting God to gently escort Him out of this world and return Him safely to His eternal home.

You can easily message American Jesus on Facebook or "friend" Him on Instagram. Nice, smiley-faced pictures and catchy Bible verses appear alongside brief, chatty messages from a few onlookers who decide to tag Him from time to time.

Maybe you've tried American Jesus and wonder if that's all there is. Maybe you, like me, feel this version of Jesus is far too plastic, disingenuous, and highly unfulfilling. Maybe snorkeling above the reef leaves *a lot* to be desired.

A DEEPER DIVE

I've made many acquaintances while traveling and encountering an extensive cross-section of the world's diverse cultures, and folks have many serious unanswered questions that inhibit faith in the Jesus of the Bible. *How do I know the Bible is true? How can I be sure Jesus is all His followers believe Him to be? How can a good God allow suffering and evil? Is the resurrection of Jesus a myth? Is Darwin or the Bible the accurate account of the origin of the cosmos and the creation of mankind? Why don't all sincere religious practices lead to heaven?*

Perhaps you've been afraid to ask the hard questions, fearing the Sunday school pictures you saw as a child might be another Santa Claus myth.

The word *scuba*, as you may know, is an acronym for "self-contained underwater breathing apparatus." Though heavy and cumbersome when strapped to your back on the side of a boat, this apparatus becomes perfectly buoyant as you dive into the ocean water below. Then *wow*! A whole new, breathtaking world opens up beneath the surface. As you dive deeply into the multicolored and textured coral reef 40 to 80 feet below, ocean life explodes before your eyes.

Day five of creation vividly leaps off the pages of the first chapter of Genesis and becomes a real-life aquarium all around you. The majestic proclamation of Genesis 1:20 is now in living color before you: "Then God said, 'Let the waters teem with swarms of living creatures.'"

Although snorkeling a safe distance above the heart,

emotions, and personality of Jesus is entertaining, wait until you put on your scuba tank and dive deeply into the relational intimacy of the "Hebrew Jesus"; the biblical Jesus; the sun-darkened, olive-skinned, brown-eyed Miracle Worker with calluses on His palms and a captivating gleam of adventure in His eyes.

There in the deep dive, where a tiger shark or manta ray may pass within your view, you will meet the Man who leveled the crowd with a tongue-in-cheek word picture of a freshly caught fish with a Roman coin in its mouth in order to answer an opportunistic Pharisee's questioning jab.

Deep in the coral reef of intimacy, you'll get to know the Man who would celebrate weddings and feasts with His disciples one moment and then who would wail deep, painful tears at a friend's funeral the next. He would place His hands softly and compassionately on the face of a little girl who had died far ahead of her time and speak a prayer that would restore vibrancy to her lifeless body. When His Father's sacred Temple was being transformed into a marketplace of mockery and defilement, those same hands would fashion whips to accompany His voice of righteous fury as He single-handedly drove an entire band of opportunistic marketeers out of His Father's place of worship and prayer.

It's the Jesus of Scripture whose heart of compassion and mercy would instantly console, restore, and forgive a woman who had turned her marital bed into marital disgrace as He boldly confronted the Jewish leadership with their hypocrisy.

Down in the Bible's oceanic depths, where the schools of colorful fish live and the coral reefs are vibrant, you'll begin to shoulder the cross beside Him as He heroically endures the excessive bloodshed of the Roman scourge and yet has the courage to carry the cross outside that tumultuous city and onto the hill of Golgotha, where He is stripped and nailed with three blacksmith spikes onto a Roman cross to receive the punishment you and I deserve for our sins.

Just last night, I was traveling in Nicaragua after spending a day encouraging my dear friends at "Amigos for Christ" in their effort to relocate families from cardboard huts in the city garbage dump into more permanent housing. And as the astonishing day came to a close, I was able to talk intimately with a Nicaraguan driver named Thomas.

On the return trip to the city, we were arbitrarily placed in Thomas's Suburban for an ever-so-short two-and-a-half-hour ride back to the Nicaraguan airport. We talked man-to-man and heart-to-heart about the "Hebrew Jesus." We put on our scuba tanks and dove deeply into Thomas's many hearsay misconceptions about the "Jesus of the Bible." Thomas had been raised by an impersonal earthly dad and lived in the crucible of conflicting "Christian" denominational interpretations of Scripture.

"Doubting Thomas" fit his mind-set well. His heart was beaten down and calloused from decades of emotional and spiritual defeat.

But as "Hebrew Jesus" came alive to him in that 150-minute encounter, he described his heart as gigantically expanding and emotionally warmed. Through tears, refreshing feelings of wonder, and previously unexperienced peace, Thomas dove deeply into a relationship he had only imagined in his wildest dreams.

As he embraced Jesus and the whole of Scripture from which His story is told, Thomas welcomed tears of joy and fulfillment that welled up behind his glasses. He wept as I gave him the Father's blessing his own dad had never extended to him. I told him how proud I was and what good I saw in him. There, in the front seat of his beat-up blue Suburban, he removed his 45-year-old "snorkel and mask" and descended deeply into the dangerously wonderful depths of knowing the Jesus of Scripture.

As we bid farewell, I embraced him as I embraced my oldest son when he made his first varsity three-point shot at the buzzer to win a highly competitive high-school basketball game.

LET'S DIVE TOGETHER

If you're ready for a deep, open-water dive and willing to shuck the familiar mask, fins, and snorkel, let's dive together! Another never-before-seen experience awaits you in the depths, where life is vibrant and colors are splashed behind every coral-laden boulder.

Like my new Nicaraguan friend Thomas, you may have to jettison some old, cumbersome baggage on the way down. Preconceived limitations, worry, fear, old scars, and precautionary walls may need to float to the surface as you descend into this adventurous wonderland. No doubt there are stingrays, sharks, and barracuda below, but as the pages of this book unfold and we unpack the truths of Scripture together, you'll find that even though predators are in the water, there is peace in their midst and enough excitement in the journey that you'll return again and again and *never* grow too old or complacent to desire more and more every day of your life.

One thing is certain. Once you go deep, you'll never want to snorkel on the surface again.

2

JUST CALL HIM DAD

THE CATALYST THAT TURNS uranium into an energy-rich nuclear fuel is fissionable neutrons. The catalyst for a gas explosion in the cylinders of a car engine is that tiny blue spark generated by the spark plug. The catalyst that turns a pregame locker room full of well-padded athletes into a ferocious football team is the sharp exhortation of a head coach's voice. The catalyst that turns a mundane, lackluster Christian experience into a vital, energizing, intimately fulfilling walk with Jesus is the realization of extraordinary love, the kind of love God offers you as your Daddy. Consider Romans 8:14-15: "For all who are being led by the Spirit of God, these are sons of God. For you have not received a spirit of slavery leading to fear again, but you have received a spirit of adoption as sons by which we cry out, 'Abba! Father!'"

Daddy love is special. Let me explain by telling you a story.

✛ ✛ ✛

My brief tenure as a Texas A&M defensive line coach meta-morphosed into a treasured, lifelong friendship with my head coach, Gene Stallings, a Bear Bryant protégé.

I joined his staff in the spring of 1971, during the final season of his Aggie coaching career. Our team won seven games and went to a bowl game, but Coach Stallings was fired at the end of the season. A few years later, he won the national championship at Alabama. He who laughs last laughs best!

Coach was and is a true hero to me. I am one of many who immensely admired this dear man and one of the fortunate few who continue to walk with him in true friendship through his retirement years. He became Bear Bryant's favorite "son" in his early days as the Bear's youngest assistant at age 23.

When I joined Coach Stallings's staff at Texas A&M, he was 36 years old, tall, handsome, and had an intimidating persona that masqueraded his tender, empathetic nature. I was going through a devastating personal loss that spring. He often sat with me and counseled me, even though he had a zillion more important things pressing into his schedule. During those emotionally devastating days, he helped me process the tragedy.

Everyone who knew Gene Stallings knew the source of his soft side. You see, Coach had four beautiful, Southern belle daughters and one winsome son named Johnny. Coach's only son couldn't count to 10, but he'd never forget your name. Soon after childbirth, the doctors told Coach and his wife, Ruth Ann, that Johnny would probably only live to age four and a half due to his many cardiopulmonary abnormalities.

When Johnny died at age 46, he had won the hearts of football fans across America. Coach and Johnny had appeared in many United Way promotional TV spots and had raised awareness and countless dollars for children with special needs.

When I heard of Johnny's passing, I rushed to the Stallingses' farm in Paris, Texas, where Coach and his wife enjoyed their retirement life with four married daughters and 11 grandchildren.

Coach was waiting for me when I entered the front door of his warm and welcoming ranch-style home. We embraced tenderly and shed tears of affection for the depth of our friendship and, of course, Johnny's life well lived.

That evening, we sat at the foot of Johnny's bed, where I listened to Coach tell the many Johnny stories that made him the star of the Arizona Cardinals, the Dallas Cowboys, and the Crimson Tide of Alabama.

Of all the Johnny stories I heard that night, there's one I will cherish forever. I wonder if Coach knew how touched I was to hear the story when he told it as if he'd never shared it before.

Each morning, Coach recounted, when he'd awaken Johnny and begin to dress him for the trip to the stadium, Johnny would look at his "best friend, Dad" and ask, "Pops, who is your favorite boy?"

Coach said he would always respond, "In the whole wide world?"

Johnny would answer, "Yes, Pops, in the whole wide world."

Coach would then say, "You are, Johnny. You are my favorite boy in the whole wide world."

Then Johnny would grin from ear to ear and say, "You know who my favorite Pop is?"

Coach would ask, "In the whole wide world?"

Johnny would answer, "Yes, in the whole wide world. You are, Pops. You are my favorite Pops in the whole wide world."

THE WAY GOD LOVES YOU

Years ago, as a young father of four small children, I learned a startling truth I first heard from my friend Hank Harmon. When a good dad has one child, he loves that child with his whole heart. No doubt, that child is his favorite in the whole wide world. Then, if that dad is fortunate enough to become the parent of a second child, his heart doubles! He loves that child with all his heart also. The second child is his favorite in the whole wide world too.

So there I found myself one late, reflective night, after a long staff-recruiting trip, walking from bedside to bedside, gazing affectionately at each of my four sleeping children whom I loved with my whole heart. Each of them was my favorite in the whole wide world.

If your affection for Jesus needs a jumpstart, if your love has grown cold or, perhaps, you find yourself stuck in a bad habit or demeaning thought pattern, please take a deep breath and listen to a catalytic truth that took me 67 years of longing to fully embrace:

Your Creator, God, has requested to be known by you as "Daddy." "Abba! Father!" Romans 8:15 testifies.

To the world, you are one in several billion. But to your Daddy in heaven, you're one of one. If I, in my limited, sinful, human nature, can be that to four children, then as omnipotent God, He can be that for you.

As His son or daughter, you must be His favorite in the whole wide world. Surely, He loves you with all His heart.

That's what good daddies do. We were made in God's

image. Genesis 1:27 proclaims this endless wonder: "God created man in His own image, in the image of God He created him; male and female He created them." Luke 11:13 hitchhikes on this truth when Jesus says, "If you then, being evil, know how to give good gifts to your children, how much more will your heavenly Father give the Holy Spirit to those who ask Him?"

So, what if you had a heart like Johnny Stallings? What if you woke up every day and looked into your heavenly Father's eyes and knew His answer when you asked rhetorically, "God, who is Your favorite in the whole wide world?"

Through the blood of His crucified Son and the sin atonement paid for by that shed blood, you can hear His reassuring voice respond, "You are. You are My favorite child in the whole wide world. I love you with all My heart!"

Ready for the fuel to explode? Ready to turn the starter on the V8 engine of your emotional and behavioral heart? Ready to place the neutrons into the nuclear reactor? If you had been the only person on earth, Jesus would have died for you. Scripture is clear: He loves you that much, and His arms are always open wide to welcome you into His embrace.

One day as I was flying from Nicaragua to Atlanta, God embraced a Nicaraguan flight attendant who had been orphaned at birth. As I befriended this woman, I learned she had no dad, no mom, no grandparents—no one to fill that "daddy" place in her heart. So I shared Jesus with her and His love of adoption, and her walk with her Father began. As we prayed together over her reassurance that Jesus was her "Dad," her heart nearly burst with tender emotion. God will adopt you, too.

Listen to the prophetic words of Isaiah as God speaks of the impending sufferings of His Son on the cross to save your soul from eternal separation: "But the LORD was pleased to crush Him, putting Him to grief; if He would render Himself as a guilt offering" (Isaiah 53:10).

The only pain worse than the nails in the hands and feet of Jesus was His thought of spending eternity without you. *Irresistible love.*

3

HIS LOVE TRANSFORMS

IN A FRIENDLY WEST TEXAS TOWN just south of the Red River, a newly constructed 12-foot cross towered behind me in a basketball arena on the university campus. I had just built it as part of my "The Cross Builder" presentation, in which I portray a Roman cross builder and talk about the Man, Jesus, who's about to be hanged on it. At the end, I invite the audience to write their sins and their pain on note cards and then come forward and pin them to the cross.

The look on Destiny's face as she tearfully and expectantly approached told a story I wanted to read and help interpret.

Her beautiful, brown eyes sparkled like the morning dew with numerous tears laced between her long, black eyelashes. I knew in an instant, as she and her friend Diane lingered before me, that she wanted to—no, she *needed* to unpack the story behind those tears that caused lines of mascara to run down her soft, brown cheeks.

Destiny was just one of thousands of students who came to the cross that morning. Each student was on a mission, a pilgrimage to find forgiveness, peace, and reconciliation or a relationship with the Man who had died on a cross 2,000 years before. In the arena, they had witnessed through me the grueling drama of the construction of the cross through the eyes of the Roman woodcutter who built it. Then, in an onstage role change, the audience experienced a taste of the passion of Jesus and His graceful, beckoning call for adoption to any willing person who would come in faith and believe.

I asked Destiny, as I had asked countless students before in 35 years of portraying that drama on campuses across the nation, to tell me her story. Without as much as a blink of her eyes, her steady gaze guided her words of a lifetime of abuse and abandonment. She described the seven-year-old girl inside her who was first assaulted by an adult family member. Then she talked of the long, dark road of sex trafficking she was forced to travel as a young teen. Her friend Diane stood shoulder to shoulder beside her, and though unwilling to tell her own story, she expressed similar feelings of heartbreaking sorrow.

I shared with her my favorite verse from the greatest love letter ever written by the greatest Lover who ever lived. With words of kind, reassuring empathy, I gently quoted 2 Corinthians 5:17: "Therefore if anyone is in Christ, he [or she] is a new creature; the old things passed away; behold, new things have come." There, in the middle of that arena filled with hundreds of students passing to and from the cross, I gently embraced Diane and Destiny as an old grandpa would embrace his granddaughters on a Christmas morning.

I shared with Destiny the biblical miracle of metamorphosis

that makes the preceding verse come alive. She drank the meaning of it deeply into her soul as a runner would drink a cold glass of water after a marathon on a hot July day. I explained the divine wonder of the process whereby a caterpillar fashions for itself a coffin to die in, a chrysalis in which it will completely deteriorate, even to the extent of the DNA of each cell decomposing to the basic amino acids from which it was made.

Destiny tracked with every word. I could see her soul sprouting wings as I explained how a dream lies inside that cocoon, a dream that reassembles the genetic dust into a brand new creation—literally a completely new species, an inexplicable scientific wonder. I saw a new Destiny emerge as I told how the beautiful, dainty butterfly will crawl out of that coffin, a creature that doesn't reflect the caterpillar from which it came.

It was as miraculous as picturing Jesus walking on water as He recreated Destiny before my eyes. The Holy Spirit performed her metamorphosis. The lovely hands of Jesus cradled her once-shredded heart and became her "chrysalis" as her old life died and the blood of Jesus transformed the caterpillar into the pristine wings of the butterfly who was ready to soar into a new life in Christ.

Destiny realized it! She beheld her personal transformation. She experienced the metamorphosis of soul offered to every sincere believer who makes his or her pilgrimage to the cross, where the death of Christ gives the life of Christ to every willing person!

I've seen hundreds of thousands of Destinys, young and old, experience the transformative life of Jesus in countries around the world. Although every story is different, the truth of the transforming power of Christ is the same.

"For the Son of Man has come to seek and to save that which was lost" (Luke 19:10).

"I once was lost, but now am found; was blind, but now I see."[1]

As Destiny walked away that morning in West Texas, I called her name and asked, "Destiny, what are you?"

Her contagious smile built a bridge across her face, and her moistened eyes nearly danced with hope. "A butterfly," she whispered. "I'm a butterfly."

GRACE AND PEACE

Grace. Oxford's dictionary defines this luminous term as "the free and unmerited favor of God, as manifested in the salvation of sinners and the bestowal of blessings."[2] Call it a gift; call it unmerited favor; call it an undeserved benefit; call it whatever you want. But when you wrap your mind around the biblical idea of a supernatural being, who is intelligent enough to invent the DNA molecule with one billion biochemical steps functioning in absolutely perfect harmony and powerful enough to speak 100 billion galaxies into existence, while being loving enough to allow a grueling, treacherous death to overtake His only Son as the atonement for *all* your and my transgressions, the simple, five-letter word *grace* soars to heights only astronauts can comprehend. As a father of two girls, I am convinced that if Destiny were the only person on earth who needed to know the miraculous, soul-healing power of grace, Jesus would have gone to the cross for her and her alone.

Peace. After "going deep" with Jesus through a blinding personal experience, 17 years of vetting the Scriptures, three perilous missionary journeys covering nearly 7,000 miles over a period of 14 years, including countless nights in prison, beatings "times without number," five Jewish scourgings of 39 lashings each, one stoning, and three beatings with rods, Paul still began almost every epistle with the words, "Grace to you and peace from God our Father and the Lord Jesus Christ."

"Grace and peace." Don't let the simplicity fool you! Consider these Scriptures: "Therefore, having been justified by faith, we have peace with God through our Lord Jesus Christ, through whom also we have obtained our introduction by faith into this grace in which we stand; and we exult in hope of the glory of God" (Romans 5:1-2).

"In Him we have redemption through His blood, the forgiveness of our trespasses, according to the riches of His grace" (Ephesians 1:7).

This is the omnipotent God who can place 10 septillion (10^{24}) stars precisely in their place; an all-knowing God who acquaints Himself with every small sparrow that takes its last breath; a holy, holy, holy God who is exceedingly more flawless than the last perfectly formed, hexagonal snowflake crystal that just fell on the 19,341-foot peak of Mount Kilimanjaro.

As it was true with Destiny, so it is with you today. May I invite you to breathe this truth deeply into your soul as you read these precious lines of Scripture from your Lord God and Creator, who declared permanent peace with you the moment Jesus cried out from the cross, "Father, forgive them; for they do not know what they are doing" (Luke 23:34).

History attests that on December 7, 1941, the Imperial Japanese Navy attacked Pearl Harbor, Hawaii, with the might of 56 warships and 353 airplanes. Beginning at 7:48 a.m., the blatantly unprepared United States naval shipyard experienced the fury of Japanese aggression. After the air assault ended, 19 ships were either sunk or severely damaged. The next day, President Franklin D. Roosevelt asked Congress for a declaration of war on Japan. For the next three years, eight months, and 25 days, the battle raged between these two world powers. But finally, on September 2, 1945, on the deck of the USS Missouri, a peace treaty was signed and the long, ugly war was over. No more bombs were dropped; no more bullets were fired; no more bloodshed; no more strife.

My dad was a gunnery officer aboard the USS Copahee, patrolling the Pacific Ocean on that historic day when the treaty was signed. Before he died, he told me about the great relief that he and all US Navy personnel experienced when word about the treaty reached the Japanese armed forces. Instantly, all fighter planes were retrieved, all artillery shells were recalled to their storage containers, and all enmity, strife, fear, and bloodshed subsided.

Today, Americans enjoy driving the Honda, the Toyota, and the Nissan as the Japanese auto companies build and sell numerous cars in the US every day. The Japanese people wear Apple watches and open Windows technology on American-made laptops. And more than a million Japanese-Americans enjoy a life of peace and security in all 50 states.

Scripture is crystal clear that at the very moment you, as a believer, sincerely trusted Jesus Christ as Lord and Savior of your life, the war between your sinful humanity and God's holy deity was over. "It is finished!" Jesus cried with His final breath (John 19:30). The peace treaty was ratified on that hill of crucifixion. The settlement between you as a true believer and God as a true Father was guaranteed and sealed in His shed blood.

Every adult in first-century Israel was all too familiar with the cruel Roman treatment of those who dared to defy its authority, which began in 63 BC when General Pompey conquered Jerusalem. According to Roman law, a prisoner would bear a "certificate of debt" with his "crimes" and terms of imprisonment written on clay tablets.

As the convicted person was cast into an iron-barred cell, this "certificate of debt" would hang on the dungeon door.

After the prescribed terms of imprisonment were satisfied, the prison guard would carve into the clay tablet the word *Tetelestai* and grant the prisoner his freedom. "Paid in full," the declaration read. The prisoner would carry with him the "terms of peace" inscribed on the tablet for the remainder of his life. If someone ever accused him again of his crime, he would produce the tablet and the declaration of peace, *Tetelestai*.

A never-to-be-forgotten moment occurred on that day of crucifixion when the Lamb of God grasped your certificate of debt in the palm of His bleeding hand and cried out in the Aramaic tongue, "*Tetelestai*." "It is finished." Jesus' divinely forgiving blood covered your hostilities against the holiness of God; your debt is paid in full; His love has prevailed over sin and death; peace has been delivered; the war is over.

Scripture describes it well in the second chapter of Colossians: "When you were dead in your transgressions and the uncircumcision of your flesh, He made you alive together with Him, having forgiven us all our transgressions, having canceled out the certificate of debt consisting of decrees against us, which was hostile to us; and He has taken it out of the way, having nailed it to the cross" (Colossians 2:13-14).

Satan, as "the accuser of the saints," constantly recreates in our minds pictures of past failures, guilt, and shame. The guilt follows us like a shadow, as the finger of the accuser points to our disappointments of previous days.

Although peace has been declared and the treaty has been ratified, almost every Christ-follower I know is terrified of the dark shadow of guilt following him or her.

But when that besieged believer lays claim to the terms of peace David expressed in Psalm 32, a gigantic feeling of relief and a sense of "peace that passes all understanding" begin to reign in the person's heart:

"How blessed is he whose transgression is forgiven, whose sin is covered! How blessed is the man to whom the LORD does not impute iniquity, and in whose spirit there is no deceit! When I kept silent about my sin, my body wasted away through my groaning all day long. For day and night Your hand was heavy upon me; my vitality was drained away as with the fever heat of summer. I acknowledged my sin to You, and my iniquity I did not hide; I said, 'I will confess my transgressions to the LORD'; and You forgave the guilt of my sin" (Psalm 32:1-5).

As a father of four children whom I've cried over countless times, invested my life into, adored, cherished, and spent a small fortune raising, I know you, as Jesus' adopted children, were on His mind the day He signed your peace agreement in His blood.

Your name was on His lips that day! He's your Creator! He's your Daddy!

"It is finished!" Your debt is paid in full. Even the shadow of guilt is erased.

"Satan lied to you once," I often say to teenagers I counsel who continually lament their sexual indiscretions of previous days. "Don't let him lie to you again."

Perhaps you, too, need a reminder today, as do I: "Grace to you and peace from God our Father and the Lord Jesus Christ" (Philippians 1:2).

Walk peacefully today. Sleep peacefully tonight. God's love cannot be denied. The peace treaty has been signed and ratified. Let His irresistible love transform you, just as it did Destiny on that unforgettable day in West Texas.

4

A TALE OF THREE TAXIS

TRULY, GOD'S IRRESISTIBLE LOVE is for all. It says in 2 Peter 3:9 that God doesn't wish for any to perish, "but for all to come to repentance." You'll see this truth come to life in my tale of three taxis.

+ + +

There are thousands of taxis and limos in Chicago. One was driven by a kindhearted Syrian-American gentleman named Imod. Another was driven by a gregarious fellow from Pakistan named Amin. Meanwhile, 1,004 miles southwest of Chicago, 1,700 limos and taxis serve Denver, Colorado, and the surrounding suburbs. There, a talkative Iranian-American named Anush drove his black GMC Denali in and out of Denver International Airport.

All three drivers were devout Muslims and had been working in America for decades. Their only knowledge of Jesus came from the scant references to Him in the Koran, as verbalized by its writer, Muhammad, in his many ethereal trances between the years AD 609 and AD 632 and recorded by the personal scribes who recorded his revelations. Some of the Koran's references to Jesus are greatly distorted, however. For example, it claims Jesus is not the Son of God (S112:2-3), that He never died on the cross (S4:157), that a substitute died for Him so there is no atonement for sin, and that He is an apostle of Allah (S4:171).

The Koran from which Amin, Anush, and Imod had been trained from their earliest days also contains conflicting statements, such as these about the duration of the creation of the cosmos: "in the twinkling of an eye" (S54:49-50), "in two days" (S941:9-12), "in four days" (S41:10), "in six days" (S7:54), "a day equaling a thousand years" (S32:5), and "50,000 years" (S70:4). While acknowledging the virgin birth of Jesus, the Koran teaches there was no crucifixion and therefore no forgiveness of sins. Muhammad also taught that disobedient wives should be banned to the couch and beaten (S4:34) and that all Jews and Christians are swine (S2:65 and S5:60).

Other teachings from the Koran are far from scriptural truth and were driven by the author's anger, his disdain for women, and his hatred of Jesus and Christians. Anush, Amin, and Imod displayed none of Muhammad's revengeful spirit, however, and overlooked many of his bitter comments.

IMOD

Imod was the first of my three unforgettable encounters. The year was 1993, during the Chicago Bulls basketball dynasty when Michael Jordan, Scottie Pippen, Will Perdue, Horace Grant, and Trent Tucker were dazzling exuberant fans with stunning dunks, signature moves, and countless three-point swishes of the net. The fabulous Bulls legends had also delivered three (at that point) NBA championships to their delighted fans.

I traveled to Chicago with my basketball-crazed 13-year-old son, Brady, to see the Jordan and Pippen matchup with David Robinson, Avery Johnson, and the highly respected San Antonio Spurs. To the shock of the silenced 18,000 Bulls fans, the Spurs won a double overtime thriller by a score of 107-102. David Robinson never left the floor. The seven-foot-tall, 236-pound United States Naval Academy graduate was an immovable mountain beneath the rim and was far too much for the Bulls to overcome.

The day after the game, Brady wanted to do a little basketball apparel shopping at NikeTown, a multi-floor, eye-opening buying adventure for any aspiring young athlete. So we grabbed a taxi for the 40-mile downtown loop, and that's where we met Imod from Syria and developed a never-to-be-forgotten friendship.

During the $60 round trip, Imod and I talked about his life in America, his family, the somewhat insane Chicago traffic, the Bulls, and the Bears. It was a delightful adventure in cross-cultural friendship.

When we arrived back at the home of my friend Steve Haas, where we were staying, I posed a respectful question to my new Syrian friend: "Imod, according to your Muslim beliefs, what will happen to you when you die?"

Imod quickly responded, "When I die, there will be judgment. As I stand before Allah, he will put all my good deeds on my right side and all my bad deeds on my left side. If my good deeds outweigh my bad deeds"—his countenance brightened—"I will go to heaven."

As he concluded, I probed, "And what if your bad deeds outweigh your good deeds?"

"Well," his countenance darkening, "I suppose I will go to hell."

"Imod," I spoke tenderly, "that worries me deeply for you."

"Because?"

"If I had to live my life worrying that if my bad deeds outweighed my good deeds I would go to hell, I would be scared to death." (Trust me, I'm not counting!)

Knowing that, under those conditions, he was paddling the same sinking boat as me, Imod returned the question to me: "What does your faith teach you?"

Our eyes were welded in earnestness as I said, "My New Testament faith clearly teaches that when I die, there will be judgment. But upon judgment, God will not look at my good deeds and compare them to my bad deeds. God will look at me based on the righteousness of Jesus Christ, who lives in my heart, and because of Him I will go to heaven."

Imod received my friendship and my faith with gratitude. "No one ever told me that before. By the way, where are you going to church tomorrow?"

I told him, and he eagerly wrote it down.

There, in that one appointed moment under the roof of that appointed taxi, God fulfilled His desire for one more Muslim man named Imod to know the Savior and experience eternal life by grace alone through faith alone in Jesus alone.

ANUSH

Fast-forward 15 years, and travel with me to the eastern slopes of the Rocky Mountains and the mile-high city of Denver, where God showed His graceful hand in an equally astonishing way. I went there to speak at an evangelical crusade on the Colorado University campus in Boulder and appear on a radio broadcast with my dear, longtime friend Dr. James

Dobson, founder of Focus on the Family. It would be a busy day filled with a backlog of phone calls between the two meetings. A driver was probably a good idea.

After arriving at Denver International, I walked to the limo and taxi pickup island, where I was met by a random limo service that had provided a shiny, black Denali for my jaunt to Colorado Springs and then up to Boulder.

Even though I've enjoyed a dozen or two radio shows with Dr. Dobson over the years, I still get a little nervous about going on the air and trying to present an idea to millions of listeners. This particular day, the butterflies in my stomach flew a little more wildly than usual because after the recording, I would have to face around a thousand students on the Colorado University campus, where Christian speakers often get harassed and scoffed at amid negative social media and school newspaper campaigns.

Stepping into the limo, I was greeted by a handsome Iranian-American gentleman named Anush. He had come to the States a decade or so before to raise his family in the nation that still remained the "land of the free and the home of the brave."

Even though he spoke in broken English with a charming Arabic flavor, and I spoke broken English with an obvious Texas flavor, we understood each other well and talked consistently for the entire four-hour loop. Actually, he talked consistently while I posed various questions and listened to his story.

As I bailed out of the Denali in Boulder and bid Anush farewell in front of the campus chapel, I honestly thought I'd never see my new friend again. (I'm still learning to never underestimate God's persistence in accomplishing His plan to "seek and to save that which was lost" [Luke 19:10] and

His quest to be "patient toward you, not wishing for any to perish but for all to come to repentance" [2 Peter 3:9].) After the speech, I returned home to Missouri.

The following Monday, I made another trip to Colorado for our AfterDark college crusade at Colorado State University in Fort Collins, just a 60-minute drive from north Denver. As I hustled out of Denver International to seize another random limo, the thought never occurred to me that God had a plan for Anush and that I was intended to be a player in the fulfillment of that plan, using a shiny, black Denali as the intended sanctuary. But guess which driver awaited me.

As I jumped into Anush's limo, we both expressed amazement over the "coincidence." We took up our conversation where we had left off the week before, with Anush talking and Joe listening. Seizing a pause in the conversation, I asked my Iranian-American friend, "Anush, what do you think of the Muslim jihad?" (This is the koranic teaching that if a Muslim kills himself in a "holy war" in the name of Allah, the suicidal Muslim gets an instant passage into heaven, where an orgy of 70 virgins awaits him [S52:17-24] [S55:54-56] [S78:32-34]).

Anush quickly responded, "I think it's baloney!"

I then asked in a friendly manner, "What do you think about the Five Pillars of Islam?" The Five Pillars are the five obligations every Muslim must satisfy to live a good and responsible life. Carrying out these obligations provides the framework of a Muslim's life and weaves his everyday activities and beliefs into a single cloth of religious devotion (Hadith of Gabriel).

"I tell you the same thing," he said. "It's baloney!"

"So you don't believe in the Koran?" I asked.

"Some of it yes, some of it no," he responded, puzzled.

The trip to Colorado State was filled with laughter and friendly conversation. As we pulled into the loading dock at the rear entrance of the hall where I would speak, a heavy, wet snow began to fall. I looked at my watch and realized I had only 25 minutes until I was up on the platform.

I turned to Anush and asked in the most-amiable manner, "Anush, you've been telling me about your faith. Would you like to know about mine?"

He readily agreed.

For the past 30 years I have carried a little Bible in my back pocket for priceless moments of opportunity like this. I reached for that gem and handed it to my Muslim friend. One by one, I had him read Revelation 4:8, Romans 3:23, Romans 6:23, Romans 5:8, and Ephesians 2:8-9. As he read each verse in a step-by-step manner, I drew two mountains, a deep valley, and a bridge across the valley that was shaped like a cross.

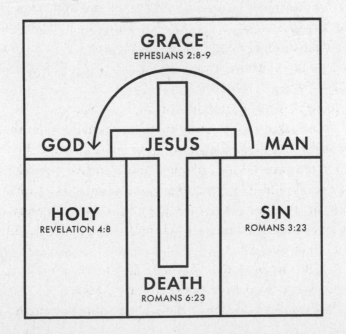

Anush studiously read and watched as I drew. It all went well until he came to Ephesians 2:8-9. That's where he buckled. I knew he would. The Koran knows nothing of grace. Muslim salvation is *all* about works and fear.

As he read, "For by grace you have been saved through faith; and that not of yourselves, it is the gift of God; not as a result of works, so that no one should boast," a puzzled scowl wrinkled his brow.

I said, "Anush, do you know what grace is?"

He said, "No."

I reached into my wallet and handed him a $20 bill. He thanked me.

I jokingly remarked, "Anush, whose $20 bill is that?"

"Mine," he said with a smile.

"How'd you get it?" I asked.

"I earned it," he responded proudly.

Jovially, I gave him *another* $20 bill and said, "But you didn't earn that! You're good, but not *that* good."

He smiled and folded the second bill.

I looked him in the eye and quickly and calmly whispered, "Anush, whose $20 bill is that?"

"Mine," he said somberly.

"How'd you get it?" I prodded.

He smiled and gratefully said, "It was a gift."

"Yes, Anush, it was a gift. That, sir, is grace. It's a gift!"

As the truth and meaning of God's amazing love landed in his heart, Anush recoiled defensively. "But with God you must obey!" he insisted. The decades of Muslim indoctrination of fear and retribution captured him again for one final round.

I never dropped my deep gaze into his eyes. "Anush," I asked calmly, "are you a dad?"

"Yes," he said proudly. "I have two boys, ages 21 and 23."

"Do you love your boys, Anush?"

"Of course I love my boys!"

I landed the final loving punch. "Anush, would you love them *less* if they were in prison?"

"My children must obey!" he retorted.

"I know," I gently followed, "but I need to know, would you love them less if they were in prison?"

"No," he said, "I would love them the same."

You could *feel* God's peace and understanding inside that limo as this dear Muslim man experienced, for the first time, the truth of our merciful Savior as boldly expressed in 2 Corinthians 6:18: "And I will be a father to you, and you shall be sons and daughters to Me, says the Lord Almighty." And ever so affectionately in Romans 8:14-16, "For all who are being led by the Spirit of God, these are sons of God. For you have not received a spirit of slavery leading to fear again, but you have received a spirit of adoption as sons by which we cry out, 'Abba! Father!' The Spirit Himself testifies with our spirit that we are children of God."

"Anush," I concluded, "the God of this Bible wants to be your dad."

His eyes expressed a supernatural peace. His words expressed thanksgiving.

AMIN

My favorite taxi ride in my nearly seven decades of life, however, came just a month before I wrote these words. This one took place just outside O'Hare Airport in Chicago at 10:30 on a cold and misty early winter night. The limo driver popped into my life as randomly as the previous two. I'm sure, as I am with the others, that the encounter was no accident. The driver's name was Amin, and he was from Pakistan. He, too, was a Muslim gentleman, probably in his early fifties. He greeted me with a beautiful ear-to-ear smile and a firm handshake.

"Welcome to Chicago," he said.

"Dude, you've got a beautiful smile," I responded. "Did your mom give you that?"

We chatted as if we'd known each other for years as we drove into the suburbs where I was to address a high school assembly the following morning.

I literally felt God pressing into my chest to go deep with Amin and journey with him into the fascinating realm of faith.

"Amin," I asked abruptly, "what will happen to your soul when you die? Teach me."

A hush fell on the interior of the limo. The silence was heavenly. I could sense the Spirit of God confronting the futility of his Muslim faith.

"I don't know," he responded. "I've never actually thought about it." He stammered pensively, "No one has ever asked me that. What do you believe?"

As it was with Imod and Anush, the observation first penned by Blaise Pascal became blatantly apparent in Amin's quest for understanding. Pascal wrote that "there is a God-shaped vacuum in the heart of every man which cannot be filled by any created thing, but only by God the Creator, made known through Jesus Christ" (*Pensées* VII[425]).

I leaned forward from the soft, leather back seat and placed my hand affectionately on Amin's shoulder the way a dad would affirm his son in a tender moment.

For the next 40 minutes, I lovingly explained to him the grace of the Jesus of the New Testament and the Father's desire to adopt every man (Ephesians 1:5).

Amin was deeply pensive. At one point he asked if I was an angel. I chuckled as I assured him I was nothing more than an ordinary man. He talked of chills permeating his body as the revelation of a loving God resonated inside his empty soul.

As we parked in front of my nighttime residence in a west Chicago suburb, I asked if he wanted to receive Christ as his Lord and Savior.

He quickly replied, "Yes, I do." He said his heart was beating rapidly. He was filled with the presence of God as he prayed sincerely to know Jesus.

I tried to give him a tip as I paid the fare. He refused my offer, saying, "You've already given me so much more."

We lingered together in the limo for another 10 minutes or so as I shared endearing Scriptures about his new Lord and Savior from the books of Colossians and John.

He said softly, "I don't want you to leave." It was 11:45 p.m.

As I got out of the limo to bid my dear friend farewell, he asked me to hug him.

There, just before midnight in the cold, misty rain on a west Chicago cul de sac, a "Hallmark moment" took place that I'll cherish forever. Two grown men hugged affectionately, like a family at a graduation ceremony in which a very proud dad would embrace a victorious son.

We didn't want to let go. It was a moment when time stood still and heaven came to earth once again.

"This is good and acceptable in the sight of God our Savior, who desires all men to be saved and to come to the knowledge of the truth" (1 Timothy 2:3-4).

Have you, like these three drivers, found God's irresistible love? Remember, God's love is for everybody. Let's talk next about how amazed we should all be by the intimate love of Jesus.

5

AN AMAZING GOD

"I am a Baptist." Fantastic!

"I am a Presbyterian." Great!

"I am a Pentecostal." Super!

"I am a Catholic." Awesome!

"I am a devout Lutheran." Cool!

"I am a sincere Methodist." Nice!

"I am an Assembly of God member." Good!

"I am a member of A.W.'s church." Okay!

"I am a Calvinist." Fine!

"I am an Arminian." Outstanding!

"I am an independent, free will, First Baptist, Second Presbyterian, Third Christian, Fourth Church of Christ." All right!

At latest count there are approximately 41,000 Christian denominations and organizations in the world—many of which, believe it or not, insist they're the *only true* way to Jesus and eternal life.[1]

Jesus said, "Follow *Me*" (Mark 1:17, emphasis added).

Intimacy is best defined as "oneness with Jesus"—just Jesus, Jesus plus nothing, simply Jesus. "Come to Me, all who are weary and heavy-laden, and I will give you rest. Take My yoke upon you and learn from Me, for I am gentle and humble in heart, and you will find rest for your souls. For My yoke is easy and My burden is light" (Matthew 11:28-30).

The fact that Jesus offers us this intimacy is amazing in so many ways. A young lady named Maggie would agree. Let me tell you her story.

+ + +

We were in the Texas Tech basketball arena with a diverse crowd of 2,300 Red Raider athletes, Greeks, geeks, and freaks. We performed "The Cross Builder" drama, and for 40 minutes you could hear a pin drop. The revival of the student body was beyond belief. Suddenly, things got out of hand for the fire marshal, who only wanted a few students on the floor at a time!

A reverent stampede erupted as the arena bleachers rapidly emptied. Broken, honest, humble, and lost students, many with tear-stained faces, paraded to the cross for a relationship, for forgiveness, for restoration, and for salvation. They wanted Jesus.

Then the unbelievable happened.

In this day of campus unrest, brokenness, party 'til you pass out, drug smorgasbord, and illicit sex of every imaginable kind, the student mob all dropped to their knees across the arena floor to humbly and reverently give their lives to Jesus.

I slipped into the crowd to provide daddy hugs and assurance to the most-hurting students, evidenced by prolific tears of repentance and relief.

I stopped in front of a petite female student with beautiful brown eyes and wavy, shoulder-length, brown hair. She sobbed profusely.

"What's your name?" I asked.

"Maggie," her trembling voice answered.

"Maggie," I responded as I gently placed my hands on the sides of her shoulders, "I already love you like a grandpa. That's my granddaughter's name! Why are you crying like that?"

She responded through more tears, "When I was 17, I died. They filmed me. The boys set me up. They stripped me and hurt me and filmed me. They made me porn."

A long, empathetic silence fell over the newly formed grandpa-granddaughter relationship.

My right hand reached into my back right pocket, where I retrieved a love letter I'd been carrying with me for several decades.

I read from its tattered, dog-eared pages, "He made Him who knew no sin to be sin on our behalf, so that we might become the righteousness of God in Him" (2 Corinthians 5:21).

Then I gently paraphrased and personalized the verse for Maggie's clear understanding. "Maggie, look! God made Jesus, who knew no sin, to become porn, become rape, become cutting, become hatred, become *everything* you've gone through so that you, Maggie, could become the purity of Jesus. Maggie, do you know what that means?"

"Help me." Her countenance lifted.

"Maggie," I comforted, "God is saying in His love letter to you tonight that when you came down to the cross and placed your trust in Jesus, He made you His bride. Maggie, you are Jesus' bride—His pure, virgin bride."

Maggie understood. She got it!

A beautiful, pure, white wedding veil fell from the ceiling of that arena onto Maggie's face. No one else saw it, of course, but Maggie did! Maggie felt it, too, and so did I. After we prayed, she turned to walk resolutely virgin-pure out of the arena. It was a bridal procession with beautiful, divinely bequeathed, dainty rose petals lying beneath her feet.

Jesus. Just Jesus. Jesus plus . . . nothing. Isn't that amazing?

ENTHRALLED

Dial back into history with me, and place yourself in Peter's sandals as Jesus called out from among the multitude those who simply "hung out" with Him and those who truly believed. As the multitudes departed, Jesus turned to the 12 and said to them, "'You do not want to go away also, do you?' Simon Peter answered Him, 'Lord, to whom shall we go? You have words of eternal life. We have believed and have come to know that You are the Holy One of God'" (John 6:67-69).

The 12 were enthralled by Jesus. To know God is to be enthralled by Him and His irresistible love. This sense of fascination can be compared to what a groom feels for his bride.

I have known my bride, Debbie-Jo, for almost 50 years and have been amazed that she has been my wife all those years. I cherish that girl. We have walked through storms together. I have long lists in my mind of her countless admirable traits. This "Cherish List," as my dear friend the late

Gary Smalley called it, goes with me through rainstorms and torrential downpours of marriage and family.

To me, our marriage is all about her. I respect, admire, and cherish every cell in her body, mind, and spirit. She studies and teaches Scripture profusely. She is consumed by God's Word. The more I see her, the more I love her. The more time I spend with her, the more I cherish her. Every day I'm married to her, I see new qualities that make me love her more.

Debbie-Jo is so far out of my league that my friends look at me and shake their heads in disbelief.

Is she the perfect wife, the perfect person, the perfect mom? Of course not. She'd probably hit me if she caught me saying "outlandish" things like this about her! But I'm enthralled with her. And the feeling of deep love I have for her is only a *mere shadow* of what it's like to know Jesus!

To know Him is to make a "Cherish List" of qualities you admire about Him and extend it every day. To know Him is to place the highest value upon Him such that no one or no thing can approach it in worth or priority. To know Him is to echo Einstein's words, "I am . . . enthralled by the luminous figure of the Nazarene." To know Him is to be *enthralled* with Him.

Knowing Jesus is being enthralled by His majesty as you look into the telescope and see the wonders of the cosmos—what Webster's dictionary defines as the "orderly, harmonious system."

Knowing Jesus is being enthralled by His brilliance as you look into the microscope and see the indescribable artistry of just one of the 125 million photoreceptors in the retina of your eye, with every cell performing 500 nonlinear differential equations 100 times every 1000th of a second (and I barely made a C in college calculus).

Knowing Jesus is being enthralled every time you see a monarch butterfly "haphazardly" dancing through the breezy fall air and recalling in astonishment that that flying miracle with a brain the size of a pinhead is on a pre-programmed journey from its mother's home in southern Canada across the United States and continuing deeply into southern Mexico, to the very tree where its great-great-great-grandfather grew up—and all without ever meeting him! Through four miraculous metamorphosis cycles traveling north and one miraculously long metamorphosis-free journey south, that tiny-winged creature, using a comprehensive climate collection system and a continental tracking system that rivals a military-grade GPS, with God-given brilliance, will find its way to its ancestral home.

With that same type of sheer amazement, one who seeks a fulfilling relationship with Jesus will dive into the Bible with the highest expectations. With that attitude of awe and wonder, one who yearns for a dynamic relationship with the Good Shepherd will wake up in the morning preparing to fill every available moment with gratitude, words of praise, and Scripture reflections woven throughout the conversations, attitudes, decisions, and relationships that each day delivers to the doorway of his or her life.

To know Him is to heed Deuteronomy's exhortation to love Him with "all your heart and with all your soul and with all your might" and to talk of His Words "when you sit in your house and when you walk by the way and when you lie down and when you rise up. You shall bind them as a sign on your hand and they shall be as frontals on your forehead. You shall write them on the doorposts of your house and on your gates" (Deuteronomy 6:5, 7-9).

A HUMBLE HEART

For me, knowing Jesus means living in sheer amazement and complete astonishment that someone as great as Him would actually love someone like me. When I consider who I was before I knew Him, how blessed I am with Him, and who I'd be without Him, all I can do is fall on my knees and worship.

It can be the same for you, wherever you are in this moment, but you'll need to be humble and recognize God's amazing character.

You'll understand this principle if you consider the lives of the kings of Judah between the years of 930 BC and 586 BC, after the nation of Israel was divided under King Solomon. In the long line of pride and corruption amongst the northern and southern kingdom kings, the atmosphere in Judah became remarkably dark under King Manasseh and the subsequent era ruled by his son Amon.

For 55 years, Manasseh "did evil in the sight of the LORD" (2 Chronicles 33:2). Furthermore, 2 Chronicles 33:6 says, "He made his sons pass through the fire in the valley of Ben-hinnom; and he practiced witchcraft, used divination, practiced sorcery and dealt with mediums and spiritists. He did much evil in the sight of the LORD, provoking Him to anger." Then his son Amon further contaminated and defiled God's chosen people as he "multiplied [his father's] guilt" (2 Chronicles 33:23).

In my many counseling experiences with men and boys of all ages, I witness repeatedly this "transgenerational curse" in which the sins of the father are passed on and become the sins of the son. Perhaps you can painfully relate as you wrestle with one or more "family traits" that seem to persist in the legacy of your own forefathers.

Before you throw in the towel, travel with me one more generation down Manasseh's family line.

Amon had a son named Josiah who must have had a good mom. Josiah could very well be you! At age eight, Josiah became king of Judah. For the next 31 years, he broke the chain of the transgenerational curse and gave you and me unforgettable insight into what it means to *know* the Lord with intimacy and fulfillment.

Scripture records that God spoke through the prophetess Huldah regarding Josiah, "'Because your heart was tender and you humbled yourself before God when you heard His words against this place and against its inhabitants, and because you humbled yourself before Me, tore your clothes and wept before Me, I truly have heard you,' declares the LORD" (2 Chronicles 34:27).

Because Josiah's heart was *tender* and he *humbled* himself, God heard him. As Josiah restored the Book of the Law, he not only lived in peace with God, but for 31 years his entire nation also followed "the God of their forefathers." Even though more than 2,600 years have passed since he was buried in the tomb, we are still singing his praises today.

A tender, humble heart that restored God's Scriptures in his life and in the life of his household was rewarded beyond his wildest dreams with a deep, abiding, fulfilling relationship with the Lord. Do you want to draw closer to this amazing God? With a humble heart, you can.

IN AWE OF YOUR ETERNAL DAD

Touring the George W. Bush museum on the Southern Methodist University (SMU) campus in Dallas, Texas, brought me to the point of tears. I sat in the September 11 Remembrance Display room with its impressive audio-visual presentation of the gallant efforts of the New York City fire-fighters during that awful day of terrorism in 2001.

Republicans, Democrats, and independents alike united that day across our nation to mourn the more than 3,000 victims of that pointless tragedy, and we have likewise mourned the 1,500 rescue workers who have died since that day, mostly due to contaminants inhaled during their heroic efforts.

Of all the displays, photos, and international souvenirs presented in that $70 million facility, I was especially impressed with an 8½" x 11" space on the wall that bore a simple letter from one of President Bush's daughters. In it she told her dad how proud she was of him. I had the chance to speak to President Bush about that letter not long after I visited, and he said it was one of his fondest possessions and greatest treasures.

Being a dad, one of the most admirable qualities I have ever observed in the people I highly esteem is the rare ability to recognize and be joyful about the accomplishments of their parents.

I was the fortunate child who grew up watching my dad love the less fortunate. We grew up in a small community in southeast Texas in the 1950s, when the racial divide in the South was deplorable. We lived mostly on the border between "colored town," as the African-American community was disrespectfully termed, and "the rest of the community." Our house, however, was not racially divided. One of my dad's best friends was Eddie Chew, a humble, elderly black gentleman who worked with him on the Texas A&M campus.

My dad worked countless hours each week for his $3,000-a-year salary. The good people "on the other side of town" clawed and scratched in desperation to feed their children and pay their heating bills.

Every Monday and Friday morning, the city garbage collectors would come to our back door at about 6:30 to empty our cans. Our family would usually be eating breakfast when we'd hear the clanging of the galvanized metal at our back door. Without fail, my dad would get up from the table, make four cups of hot coffee, place four hot biscuits or sweet rolls on a plate, and meet the four grateful African-American garbage collectors, otherwise unnoticed and unappreciated for their consistent, daily contribution to our community.

One of the utter thrills of my life was to watch my dad (after his "retirement") as he led our tiny "Ozark Hillbilly" construction team in the engineering and building of a series of urban youth camps, now affectionately known by city kids across this nation as "Kids Across America." Even though Dad has long since gone to spend eternity with the Savior he loved the most, the work of his hands continues to attract and become a place of spiritual refuge for 7,000 inner-city children each summer who get to leave the concrete walls and highways and experience "the summer of their lives" on the shores of Table Rock Lake in southwest Missouri.

As my immeasurable respect and admiration for my dad continues to grow each year, I'm reminded that my "eternal Dad" deserves that same sheer amazement and so much more. If your deepest desire is to see your faith explode as your intimacy with Jesus ascends to new heights, *stand in awe* of your Creator. Put to death any traces of entitlement that may have followed you into adult life. When life is challenging, rejoice. When life is peaceful, rejoice. Inhale gratitude with every breath. Exhale praise with every beat of your heart. Place a granite signpost in the pathway of your daily walk: "God is good all the time. All the time, God is good."

Psalm 8:3-6, 9 expresses sheer amazement well: "When I

consider Your heavens, the work of Your fingers, the moon and the stars, which You have ordained; what is man that You take thought of him, and the son of man that You care for him? Yet You have made him a little lower than God, and You crown him with glory and majesty! You make him to rule over the works of Your hands; You have put all things under his feet. . . . O Lord, our Lord, how majestic is Your name in all the earth!"

6

GOD'S MESSAGE FOR YOU

Premed biology and college football are not generally known as Siamese twins. Nor are the two ever-so-demanding ways of life compatible with a student of less than premed intellect or an athlete with less than blue-chip talent. The many sessions in the biology lab and the consistent long practices on the gridiron usually force one of the two off the schedule.

I guess I was too entrenched in both to kiss one good-bye, or maybe I just didn't know where else I'd turn.

As my biology and humanistic chemistry teachers captured more and more of my brain, my brilliant but scripturally jaded religion teacher vacated more and more of my heart. By the time I graduated from college, I was a full-blown evolutionist and intellectually steeped in Darwinism.

I didn't have biblical apologetics in my repertoire and had never heard the term *intelligent design*. No one had ever reasoned with me about the countless fallacies and unproved assumptions found in the metaphysical dogma of the so-called "Big Bang" and the accidental, random inception of life on planet earth.

That was, until I listened to one debate between a brilliant Christian biology professor and an atheistic scientist in a recorded encounter on the Berkeley campus. For one hour, the biblically based professor intellectually destroyed the naturalistic theory of mindless evolution and the one who fumbled through his arguments for his antiquated, humanistic theory.

During the 40 years that have followed that watershed moment in my life, I've become an avid student of the countless scientists who devoutly adhere to the Genesis 1 view of the inception of the cosmos, the origin of life, and the vast diversity of life on planet earth. The truths they describe reveal another facet of God's irresistible love for us.

Dr. Robert Jastrow, the past president of the NASA Goddard Institute for Space Studies, brought the naturalistic Big Bang idea to its knees when he spoke out boldly in defense of the theistic view of the origin of the cosmos:

> Most remarkable of all is the fact that in science,
> as in the Bible, the world begins with an act of
> creation. Now we see how the astronomical evidence
> leads to a Biblical view of the origin of the world.
> For the scientist who has lived by his faith in the
> power of reason, the story ends like a bad dream. He
> has scaled the mountains of ignorance; he is about
> to conquer the highest peak; as he pulls himself over
> the final rock, he is greeted by a band of theologians
> who have been sitting there for centuries.[1]

Renowned Stanford theoretical physicist Dr. Andrei Linde echoed Dr. Jastrow's words when he said, "The 'Big Bang' theory is scientifically brain dead."[2]

Nobel Laureate and Harvard physics professor Dr. Arthur Compton said of the Genesis 1 account of the divine creation of the cosmos, "For myself, faith begins with the realization that a supreme intelligence brought the universe into being and created man. It is not difficult for me to have this faith, for it is incontrovertible that where there is a plan, there is intelligence—an orderly, unfolding universe testifies to the truth of the most majestic statement ever uttered—'In the beginning, God . . .'"[3]

Webster's Dictionary actually defines the word *cosmos* as an "orderly, harmonious systematic universe."[4] Have you ever seen an explosion somehow create "order," "harmony," or anything "systematic"?

Where there is a painting, there must be a painter. Where there's a photo, there must be a photographer. Where there's a design, there must be a designer. Where there is creation, there must be a creator.

Psalm 19:1 says, "The heavens are telling of the glory of God." The more you examine the evidence, the more you stand in awe of *the One* who dreamed it, designed it, and spoke it into being, and the more you can agree with Psalm 8:1: "O Lord, our Lord, how majestic is Your name in all the earth, who have displayed Your splendor above the heavens!"

"In the beginning God created the heavens and the earth" (Genesis 1:1).

The more you marvel at the incarnate personality of the creation, namely Jesus Christ Himself, the more you want to pursue Him, study Him, worship Him, and draw close to Him.

The apostle Paul, in divinely inspired authorship, dug

deeply into the DNA of Jesus the Messiah, the Anointed One, and "the Way, the Truth and the Life":

> He is the image of the invisible God, the firstborn of all creation. For by Him all things were created, both in the heavens and on earth, visible and invisible, whether thrones or dominions or rulers or authorities—all things have been created through Him and for Him. He is before all things, and in Him all things hold together. He is also head of the body, the church; and He is the beginning, the firstborn from the dead, so that He Himself will come to have first place in everything. For it was the Father's good pleasure for all the fullness to dwell in Him, and through Him to reconcile all things to Himself, having made peace through the blood of His cross; through Him, I say, whether things on earth or things in heaven.
>
> COLOSSIANS 1:15-20

John, the disciple, described Jesus' omniscience by using the Greek term *logos* (the Word) to identify His all-knowing and timeless nature: "In the beginning was the Word, and the Word was with God, and the Word was God. He was in the beginning with God. All things came into being through Him, and apart from Him nothing came into being that has come into being" (John 1:1-3).

Jesus, as the Incarnate Man of the Trinity, was there at the beginning. He, in that triune Godhead, was the designer and creator of everything tangible and intangible, both the micro and the macro. The marvel of His creation is magnified in the microscope and beheld in the telescope.

While visiting planet Earth for 33 revealing years, He verified the first chapter of Genesis and its account of the divine creation of the cosmos and the immediate creation of man.

"But from the beginning of creation, God made them [Adam and Eve] male and female" (Mark 10:6).

In 1859, Charles Darwin, with a definite chip on his shoulder toward the Bible and the person of Jesus, changed the rules of science. Instead of true, observable, and empirical scientific evidence, Darwin's science teaches theory as fact, impossible probability as reality, and science fiction as scientific truth. Darwin wrote, "I had gradually come, by this time, to see that the Old Testament . . . was no more to be trusted than the sacred books of the Hindus or the beliefs of any barbarian. . . . I can indeed hardly see how anyone ought to wish Christianity to be true."[5]

In his book *On the Origin of Species*, Darwin based his entire mythical philosophy on one statement with four basic assumptions, all four of which have been clearly disproved in the laboratories of physics, mathematics, biology, chemistry, and cosmology. That statement was this: "Matter is eternal. All the material in the universe is the result of chance arrangements of atoms responding to known physical and chemical laws. Life arose from nonliving matter. The diversity of living systems is the result of random mutations acted upon by natural selection."[6]

GRANDEUR AND WONDER

But imagine a being so powerful that He could "speak 100 billion galaxies" that would expand over a billion light years in the first trillionth of a second; so magnificent that He could fine-tune the cosmos to the trillion, trillion, trillionth degree of perfection; so intelligent that He could pack the brilliance and complexity of the space shuttle into each of the 100 trillion cells in your body; so humble that He would clothe Himself as a servant and wash the feet of His followers; and yet so committed to relationships that He would endure the torturous flogging of the Roman government and subject Himself to six grueling hours of death by crucifixion!

Now imagine that God-Man praying for you (Romans 8:27), adopting you into His family (Romans 8:23), sealing your salvation by His Holy Spirit (Ephesians 1:13), canceling your certificate of debt (Colossians 2:12-14), and sending His Holy Spirit to you as a pledge of your eternal inheritance (2 Corinthians 5:5). And then, if that doesn't fill every place in your body, mind, and soul with grandeur and wonder, He gives you confident access (Hebrews 4:16) to the throne of grace where you can commune, have fellowship with, and know and love "the breadth and length and height and depth" of the one true God!

Can anything compare? Can anything more deeply satisfy? Can anything more completely fulfill? Can anything motivate love more richly? Can anything more completely beckon someone to draw near and pursue with reckless, sacrificial abandonment?

Perhaps the great playwright William Shakespeare said it best: "Jesus is my Saviour, my Hope, my Creator. Apart from His mercy I have no hope for eternal life. I commend my soul into the hands of God, my Creator, hoping and assuredly believing, through the only merits of Jesus Christ, my Saviour, to be made partaker of life everlasting."[7]

The psalmist wrote, "When I consider Your heavens, the work of Your fingers, the moon and the stars, which You have ordained; What is man that You take thought of him, and the son of man that You care for him? Yet You have made him a little lower than God, and You crown him with glory and majesty!" (Psalm 8:3-5).

THE FAILINGS OF EVOLUTION

Regarding his now-laughable theory of spontaneous generation that claims life on earth originated randomly through unguided chemical accidents in some "prehistoric biological soup" some 3 to 4.5 billion years ago, even the outspoken twentieth-century atheist Carl Sagan said it had only "one chance in ten to the two-billionth power of success."

Mathematician Dr. Larry Campbell said, "That possibility was about as remote as the odds of filling up a football stadium with 25 million dice, exploding it and discovering that every die in the pile had landed on the number six."

Sir Fred Hoyle, the British mathematician, knighted by the queen for his achievements in scientific research, said, "The notion that not only the biopolymer but the operating program of a living cell could be arrived at by chance in a primordial organic soup here on the Earth is evidently nonsense of a high order."[8]

Regarding Darwin's theory of progressive mutations that slowly transform a species of a more-simple design into a species of more-complex design, a growing number of dissidents in the upper echelon of the scientific community are coming out of the closet. According to Dr. C. P. Martin, "Almost all known mutations are unmistakably pathological." That is to say, 999 out of 1,000 mutations actually kill the organism rather than transform that species into a rare intelligent form.[9]

Dr. Pierre-Paul Grassé, the past president of the French Academy of Sciences, put the nail in the coffin for this "daydream" of Darwin and his many followers: "No matter how numerous they may be, mutations do not produce any kind of evolution. There is no law against daydreaming, but science must not indulge in it."[10]

Dr. Soren Lovtrup, the renowned biologist and professor of zoophysiology from the University of Sweden, tried to bring scientific reason back to the classroom when he stated, "I believe that one day the Darwinian myth will be ranked the greatest deceit in the history of science. When this happens, many people will pose the question, 'How did this ever happen?'"[11]

To Darwin's credit, science agrees that Galapagos Island *finches* can adapt different-sized beaks to become a slightly different form of *finch*. *Dogs* can similarly adapt over the years, under changing conditions, to become different forms of *dogs*. And *peppered moths* can adapt into different-colored *peppered moths*. That's called *adaptation*. But because of a God-ordained "DNA code barrier" within the composition of cells, species cannot, will not, and never have evolved into higher forms.

Dr. Colin Patterson, the once-senior paleontologist at the Natural History Museum in London, said, "No one has ever produced a species by mechanisms of natural selection. No one has even gotten near it."[12]

The historical proof lies in the fossil record. Darwin believed in gradual evolution from species to species through mutations and natural selection. Simple cells evolved into complex swimming flagellum, which evolved into jellyfish, which evolved into vertebrate fish, which evolved into amphibians, which evolved into reptiles, which evolved into birds and furry creatures, which evolved into monkeys, which became man. And so he believed that in the years following his death, science would discover countless "missing links" as one species had evolved into a higher form. Darwin said,

"The number of intermediate and transitional links between all living and extinct species must have been inconceivably great."[13]

Unfortunately for his theory, a century and a half later, with the exception of a pitifully few fallible, conjured-up, and highly exaggerated examples, exhaustive archaeology hasn't found *any* such missing links.

Dr. Colin Patterson, known throughout the world as one of the most-respected fossil scientists who ever lived, noted in his book *Evolution: No Missing Links* that a letter was mailed to him by aerospace engineer Luther D. Sunderland, author of *Darwin's Enigma*, which questioned his lack of recorded transitional forms. Dr. Patterson responded, "I fully agree with your comments on the lack of direct illustration of evolutionary transitions In my book. If I knew of any, fossil or living, I would certainly have included them. . . . I will lay it on the line; there is not one such fossil for which one might make a watertight argument."[14]

In short, an omnipotent God created you in love, crafted a universe in which you could live and journey with Him, and beckons you every minute of every day to know more of Him and His relentless love for you.

PART TWO

KNOWING GOD'S IRRESISTIBLE LOVE

7

MOVING CLOSER TO GOD

James 4:8 says, "Draw near to God and He will draw near to you." My dad taught me what it means to "draw near" to the one you love most. Let me tell you about how he did that.

+ + +

My dad was 88 years old when he died. For the last month of his life, he neither ate more than a morsel of food nor drank more than a sip of water. His left arm was functionally paralyzed due to a recent stroke. His knuckles on both hands were greatly enlarged from years of accumulative arthritis. His only activity was writing Mom love letters.

Day after day, he sat in the old, blue chair he had lived in for most of the last two years. There he wrote repetitive love notes to his only love with a blue ballpoint pen on a yellow legal pad cradled affectionately on his lap. For 66 years he wrote his bride expressive letters of his love, admiration, and devotion. During the last 20 or so years of his life, he'd write her almost daily unless he was traveling or living on the construction site of one of the many youth camps he engineered and led in the building process.

In his days of mobility, he'd wake up at 5:30 a.m., grab a bowl of cereal, and place a yellow sticky note on the kitchen counter next to Mom's coffee cup with a few endearing lines as a wake-up greeting. Then he'd march through the early-morning darkness straight to her office in the little cabin in the woods where she spent her days balancing the books. There he'd turn on her light and the small space heater by her desk, so her arrival at 8:00 a.m. would be warm and cozy.

In all my years of knowing my dad, I never heard him say a negative word about Mom. He bragged on her beauty well into his late eighties. He was absolutely certain she was the most beautiful woman in the world, and he would often say he was the "luckiest man alive" to be married to the mother of his three sons and the hero of his dreams.

Just before Daddy died, he subconsciously took Mom's hand in the withered palms of *both* his arthritic hands and strangely overcame the paralysis from which his left arm suffered. He raised her hand high above his head as if to tell Jesus, "You can take me home now, but I don't travel alone. My wife and I go together."

Do you go together with Jesus? *Draw near to God and He'll draw near to you.* What a promise from an all-powerful being who can speak a word and the entire cosmos, spanning 27.4 billion light years, not only explodes from His mouth, but in so creating it He organizes and harmoniously "tunes it" like a radio to the trillion, trillion, trillionth degree of perfection!

"Come to My side, and I'll come near your side."

"Sit by Me, and I'll sit by you."

"Hold My hand, and I'll hold yours."

"Bring Me your heart, and I'll bring you Mine."

"Hug Me like a tender and loving dad, and I'll hug you like a tender and loving son."

"Love Me like a trusting little girl loves her daddy, and I'll always love you like daddy's little girl."

"Lay your head on the pillow in your bed, and I'll put My head next to yours."

"Put your shoulder next to Mine, and I'll place My shoulder next to yours."

"Whisper your deepest longing into My ear, and I'll whisper Mine into yours."

"Share with Me your words of highest expectation and admiration, and I'll share Mine with you."

Listen to the prophet Isaiah's reassuring words: "Seek the LORD while He may be found; call upon Him while He is near. Let the wicked forsake his way and the unrighteous man his thoughts; and let him return to the LORD, and He will have compassion on him, and to our God, for He will abundantly pardon" (Isaiah 55:6-7).

And hear what 2 Chronicles 15:1-2 has to say about moving closer to God: "Now the Spirit of God came on Azariah the son of Oded, and he went out to meet Asa and said to him, 'Listen to me, Asa, and all Judah and Benjamin: the LORD is with you when you are with Him. And if you seek Him, He will let you find Him; but if you forsake Him, He will forsake you.'"

To the vast majority of students and adults I've encountered over the years, the idea of drawing near to God seems daunting, elusive, mysterious, or even sadly impossible.

Perhaps you would like to dig deeper into His magnificent invitation. Perhaps your soul, like the apostle Paul's, yearns for the more intimate connection he described in his letter to the Philippians: "That I may know Him and the power of His resurrection and the fellowship of His sufferings, being conformed to His death" (3:10).

Fortunately, God does not leave us longing without fulfillment, seeking without His response, or searching vainly for this intimate connection. His promise to respond to our "drawing near to Himself" with His "drawing near to us" is fulfilled as we invest our very lives and follow His scriptural mandate.

If you share my deep desire for the greatest relationship adventure of the entire human experience, walk with me through a dozen passages of Scripture that offer an illuminating passageway into the Father's heart.

Jesus opens himself to be known intimately by the sincere believer who is willing to heed the fullness of the simply stated truth in Matthew 5:8, "Blessed are the pure in heart, for they shall see God."

In the electronic jungle in which the modern Western world has become immersed, this prerequisite for intimacy with the Savior has little appeal to the timid who are not willing to commit fully to God, the nonsacrificial, and the materialistically addicted.

"Seek first His kingdom and His righteousness," Jesus cried out in His Sermon on the Mount by the Sea of Galilee (Matthew 6:33).

If you diligently seek Him (see Hebrews 11:6), His divine love is meant to fill and satisfy your eyes and ears; your senses of smell, taste, and touch; as well as the pathways to your heart, your mind, and your soul. *This* is where intimacy takes place. It is all of Him in all of you.

In contrast, a heart filled with porn, lust, repetitive electronic media impulses, and materialistic desire cannot keep good company with the presence of His holiness. As surely as oil will separate from water, the heart filled with what the Bible calls "the world, the lust of the flesh and the lust of the eyes and the boastful pride of life" (1 John 2:16) will not comingle with the ever-savory fulfillment of the "Holy One of Israel."

TWO HEART CONDITIONS

For four eye-opening years, I hosted a live, call-in radio broadcast with Focus on the Family. We counseled teenagers who tuned in on 325 radio stations across North America concerning difficult issues they faced in their ever-decaying youth culture. In that time I learned there are two types of heart conditions that either repel intimacy with Jesus or enhance it.

After those high-energy radio days, I encountered hundreds of thousands of men in a 10-year stint with Promise Keepers, where I was blessed to give dozens of Friday night messages calling men to repentance and surrender at the cross.

As the men would pour out of the bleachers to the arena floor of surrender, I had a rare vantage point to embrace them in their hour of decision and brokenness. As you might imagine, I discovered during those years that human nature is exactly like student nature.

Even as I speak at women's events and tread in healthy fear, I am impressed that a woman's heart is built with the same set of needs.

I'm certainly no expert with either group, but after 40 years of counseling, I've discovered that *any* human heart can be conditioned *for* intimacy with the Savior or *against* it.

The first heart condition is what I call the "iHeart." The iHeart has an "external entry road" and an "internal entry road." The *external* road has five avenues: sight, touch, taste, smell, and hearing. This road is mostly traveled through "iDevices" (e.g., iPhones, iPods, iPads, computers, and TV). Basically, it's the electronic traffic that finds its way through your eyes and ears into the billions of nerve synapses and brain cells that transport and store every single image that enters the eye gate and ear gate of the "throne room" of your life. The Greeks called this "throne room" the *cardia*, "the volitional center where life makes up its mind." The Bible calls this command post the "heart."

Your heart is spoken of some 736 times in Scripture, more than any other body part. The spiritual condition of a person's heart determines the quality of his or her life and the location of his or her eternity.

Listen carefully to Jesus' words of wisdom: "The eye is the lamp of the body; so then if your eye is clear, your whole body will be full of light. But if your eye is bad, your whole body will be full of darkness. If then the light that is in you is darkness, how great is the darkness!" (Matthew 6:22-23).

In contrast, the *internal* road of the iHeart is heavily traveled by thoughts of bitterness, unresolved anger, hatred, jealousy, pride, and self-centeredness. Proverbs 23:7 says it this way: "For as he thinks within himself, so he is."

According to Dr. Earl Nightingale, all psychologists agree on only one thing: "You become what you think about."[1] A heart that won't forgive holds no room for intimacy with Jesus. Dr. Gary Smalley said, "Bitterness is a poison pill you take thinking it's going to hurt the other person." The unforgiving heart kills marriages, parent-child relationships, and the peace of knowing God with tender fondness.

I encountered a severely wounded and bitter 14-year-old camper at our teenage sports camp after teaching a message on biblical apologetics. She was one of dozens of young girls I've encountered over the years carrying the same tragic scar. She walked up to me with two friends and said, "When I was eight, I was sexually abused by my cousin. I can't get rid of the pain."

I listened empathetically and shared with her how I took the sexual abuse I received from a strange man in my eight-year-old boyhood and carefully placed it in one of the wounds Jesus received on the cross. I gently assured her that Jesus' promise in Isaiah 53 and 1 Peter 2 had been fulfilled as I consistently placed that wound on my heart into His open wounds of healing.

"But He was pierced through for our transgressions, He was crushed for our iniquities; the chastening for our well-being fell upon Him, and by His scourging we are healed" (Isaiah 53:5).

"He Himself bore our sins in His body on the cross, so that we might die to sin and live to righteousness; for by His wounds you were healed" (1 Peter 2:24).

The next day, a completely different girl in the same human body approached me with a smile that had miraculously replaced the scowl on her face the day before. "I did what you told me," she joyfully exclaimed. "It worked! I gave it to Jesus, and He healed me."

With some individuals, the process of resolving traumatic hurt requires long periods of professional counseling. The duration of the process varies from case to case, but at the end of the day, Jesus' words of resolution and reassurance remain true. His shed blood is sufficient to heal a wounded person when, and *only* when, the victim's heart is *ready* and *willing* to truly and completely let Him take it into His wounded side to heal, restore, and rebuild.

At one of our "AfterDark" campus events a few years ago, six thousand students at Texas A&M surrounded the cross one October night, bringing the scars and transgressions they had written on 4″ x 6″ cards to the grace-filled, outstretched arms of Jesus. One passionately tearful student pointed to her card and cried, "What do I do with this?" The card read, "J.D., you killed my dad. He was my best friend."

I was filled with sorrow for her. I was silent. I simply pointed to the cross, where thousands of cards were being nailed to the pine beams. The girl looked at the cross and then back to the painful words on her card. Again, her eyes moved to the cross and back to the card. Her friends surrounded her, and I felt a massive sigh of relief when she wrote on the back of her card, "I forgive you, J.D." Resolutely, she nailed the card to the cross and walked away in easily recognizable freedom.

Jesus puts a high premium on our willingness to vacate the paralyzing inward road of the "iHeart." For those of us who have been deeply wounded, the battle to repave the roads of our heart is difficult, but it's a fight we must win!

"For if you forgive others for their transgressions, your heavenly Father will also forgive you. But if you do not forgive others, then your Father will not forgive your transgressions" (Matthew 6:14-15).

Reprogramming both the "external and internal" roads to the heart is life's greatest challenge, but in completing it, an individual receives life's greatest rewards.

NEVER AGAIN

The human will is the most powerful "muscle" in the physique of any man or woman. Jesus calls it the place where His Spirit resides. Your will is the quarterback of the football huddle, the captain of the drill team, the libero of the volleyball team, the CEO of the corporation. The will calls the plays. The will says yes and no.

A neurosurgeon locates the will in the hypothalamus of the lower central brain. This pearl-sized structure influences hormone releases that relate to a broad range of neurological and physiological processes.

Recently, at an NFL pregame chapel, I spoke to a famous Super Bowl-bound wide receiver about how his will was being treated like the tiny muscle on his little pinkie. Although married, he was watching porn, and like so many pornographically bound men I counsel, he felt hopelessly enslaved.

The athlete ran the 40-yard sprint in 4.4 seconds and bench-pressed almost 350 pounds, but his will was atrophied. He was letting his undernourished will crush his wife and destroy his marital intimacy.

I met with the player on two different occasions before two Sunday afternoon games. During the first meeting, his heart was "touched." He was motivated to change his iHeart into a "Jesus heart." He was exhausted from his entrapment.

One year later, we met again. I said to him, "Jarod [fictitious name], how is your journey with porn?"

He blinked and said, "Definitely getting better."

I responded, "Better?"

"Yes," he said confidently, "much improved."

"So . . ." I persisted, "you okay with cheating on your wife?"

"No."

"So what happened to your will? Where is Jesus in this? What about the power of the Holy Spirit?" I loved him as a good father would love his son. I was proud of his first step (as George MacDonald wrote) but never satisfied until he obtained a solid, manly walk.

Jarod wanted purity; I wouldn't settle for anything less. Purity isn't pure until the contaminants have been completely eradicated.

I continued to exhort, "Jarod, I invite you to give the Holy Spirit control of your will. I invite you to invoke the power of the One who 'spoke the cosmos' to take charge of your will."

His eyes filled with hope and conviction.

"Jarod, I invite you to utter the most powerful two-word prayer a follower of Christ will ever pray. I invite you to pray, 'Never again.'"

Jarod grabbed that prayer without any hesitation or lack of confidence in God's ability to conquer anything and everything He pleases. "Never again, Lord," he prayed. "I'll never view porn again. I promise my wife, and I promise my kids. I'm finished. I'm done."

Later that season, in a second-round playoff game, Jarod was the star of the team. Better yet, after he unleashed the power of the Spirit-controlled will, he remained a star to his wife and kids at home.

The Spirit-filled will is the key to a transformed heart.

THE JESUS HEART

In contrast to the iHeart, the rare heart—the inspired heart, the fulfilled heart, the intimate heart—is what I call "the Jesus heart." Here, He is your first love. He is your number-one priority.

"Listen carefully to Me, and eat what is good, and delight

yourself in abundance. Incline your ear and come to Me. Listen, that you may live" (Isaiah 55:2-3).

In the magnificent book *The Heartmath Solution*, by cardiologists Doc Lew Childre and Howard Martin, years of research bear testimony that a heart of grace can actually be "amped up" in the same way an iPhone is charged from a 110-volt wall outlet. The research shows that a graceful heart, which exhibits qualities of tenderness and peace, can be charged and recharged when the owner is thankful, forgiving, nonjudgmental, and caring. But when the heart is bitter, judgmental, ungrateful, self-absorbed, or controlling, it loses its potential for happiness and peace.

The psalmist wrote of the Jesus heart, "Bless the LORD, O my soul, and all that is within me, bless His holy name" (Psalm 103:1).

"I will extol You, my God, O King, and I will bless Your name forever and ever. Every day I will bless You, and I will praise Your name forever and ever. Great is the LORD, and highly to be praised, and His greatness is unsearchable" (Psalm 145:1-3).

At our Christian sports camp, we call the Jesus heart the "I'm Third" heart: God first, others second, and "I'm Third."

The Jesus heart keeps the apostle Paul's exhortation well: "Do you not know that your body is a temple of the Holy Spirit who is in you, whom you have from God, and that you are not your own? For you have been bought with a price: therefore glorify God in your body" (1 Corinthians 6:19-20).

The Jesus heart is discerning and disciplined. It says no to media engagement that is lewd or profane. The Jesus heart won't let the sun go down on its anger. It can't wait to forgive. It's not motivated by self-fulfillment or unnecessary material possessions.

This most hopeful reality is one I've observed countless times in the lives of men and women, young and old. The truth is that any repentant, broken, and sincerely believing heart can be completely transformed into a Jesus heart by an unbridled desire to engage with the Holy Spirit's power to forgive, cleanse, and heal. As the apostle Paul wrote to the Philippians, "One thing I do: forgetting what lies behind and reaching forward to what lies ahead, I press on toward the goal for the prize of the upward call of God in Christ Jesus" (Philippians 3:13-14).

Commercials for new drugs fill our TV screens. The only thing more difficult to discern than the drugs' funny names is the endless list of potential side effects. I appreciate the warnings!

The only "drug" you can get over the counter at your desk at work, your bed at home, your desk at school, or the kitchen tabletop is forgiveness. And there are no negative side effects!

A heart cleared of the rubble of bitterness heals more diseases than any pharmaceutical ever invented. The emotional infirmity that lingering bitterness causes transforms into psychological sickness like a slow-growing brain tumor.

The famous Mayo Clinic medical team released a study on the healing power of forgiveness and noted the following:

"Letting go of grudges and bitterness can make way for happiness, health, and peace. Forgiveness can lead to:

- Healthier relationships
- Greater spiritual and psychological well-being
- Less anxiety, stress and hostility
- Lower blood pressure
- Fewer symptoms of depression

- Stronger immune system
- Improved heart health"[2]

HOW TO FORGIVE

Forgiveness is consummated when you take five positive steps in prayer.

First, take the offense to Jesus on the cross. Let Him carry it. Let Him heal it. Let Him own it. His crucified body was sufficient for *all* offenses. It's not a matter of "giving it up" or "letting it go." It's all about entrusting the offense to the One who judges righteously, who can carry the load, whose outstretched arms embrace your pain, who can understand your pain, and whose shed blood heals your pain.

Second, imagine your perpetrator lying in a hospital bed, dying from cancer. While his or her cancer is not visible on a CT scan, that person who hurt you has a cancer of the heart and perhaps the deadliest illness, cancer of the soul.

Third, envision Jesus as your role model. Observe His suffering. Feel the ripping of His flesh with the Roman scourge. Try to imagine the nails being pounded into His hands and feet. Then truly hear His cry that shook the walls of Jerusalem, "Father, forgive them, for they do not know what they are doing."

Fourth, embrace the premium He placed on forgiveness as He cried out from the mount on the shore of the Sea of Galilee, "For if you forgive others for their transgressions, your heavenly Father will also forgive you. But if you do not forgive others, then your Father will not forgive your transgressions" (Matthew 6:14-15).

When I consider all He has forgiven me for, it is so easy to forgive others for the few offenses they have committed against me.

Fifth, the final shovel of dirt filling the gaping hole that bitterness causes in the graveyard of complete forgiveness is to begin to pray for your offender. "But I say to you, love your enemies and pray for those who persecute you," Jesus proclaimed (Matthew 5:44).

See that person in heaven, completely healed of his or her heart cancer that caused the affliction. Don't let Satan continue his victory march in your life! When you forgive, he is defeated.

I have tremendous respect for my first wife and my dear friend who fell in love with her more than 45 years ago, but their emotional entanglement gave me the first true test of my adult life in biblical forgiveness. I have never blamed either of them for the divorce or their love for each other. No pornography or adultery was involved in her decision. She simply fell in love with another man. Yes, I was devastated. Yes, she deserved a more mature man and better spiritual leader than I was able to provide her. Yes, I was a total wreck when she left. For three long, painful months, I felt as if I were dying. I was positive I was the biggest failure on the face of the earth.

By God's grace alone, anger and bitterness were never an option. You see, emotions are like a restaurant, but attitudes are like a smorgasbord. Sadness, happiness, excitement, and feelings of cuddly affection are delivered to your table by the server of life's ups and downs; laughter and tears are cleansing. They come and go.

Attitudes, however, are served cafeteria style. You can put on your plate whatever you choose. Love is a decision. *Hear me, husbands and wives!* Overnight anger is a decision. Bitterness is a decision. Hatred is a decision.

Yes, those attitudes presented themselves piping hot and spicy when she told me she was in love with my best friend and when the divorce papers were served. I couldn't change her, but I had a lot of work to do on me.

I have chosen to guard my "cafeteria tray" as it passes down the smorgasbord of emotions like an armed Marine with a large German Shepherd by his side. From the day my two best friends left together, I have chosen love, joy, and peace toward them. We will enjoy all of eternity together living in complete harmonious friendship. I long for that day!

Listen to the words of the inspired writer of Hebrews describing my hero and role model as He took His "cafeteria tray" down the smorgasbord of attitudes: "Therefore, since we have so great a cloud of witnesses surrounding us, let us also lay aside every encumbrance and the sin which so easily entangles us, and let us run with endurance the race that is set before us, fixing our eyes on Jesus, the author and perfecter of faith, who for the joy set before Him endured the cross, despising the shame, and has sat down at the right hand of the throne of God" (Hebrews 12:1-2).

THE POWER OF GOD'S WORD

Above all else, the Jesus heart can also be "amped up," like applying jumper cables on a car's dead battery, by memorizing and meditating on God's Word.

"How blessed is the man who does not walk in the counsel of the wicked, nor stand in the path of sinners, nor sit in the seat of scoffers! But his *delight* is in the law of the LORD, and *in His law he meditates day and night.* He will be like a tree firmly planted by streams of water, which yields its fruit in its season, and its leaf does not wither; and in whatever he does, he prospers" (Psalm 1:1-3, emphasis added).

Even though it's no secret, it is perhaps the most neglected treasure ever provided—God's promise of incredible blessings to the true believer who gives a lifelong pledge to His marvelous decree: "But his delight is in the law of the LORD, and in His law he meditates day and night" (Psalm 1:2).

Memorizing and meditating on God's Word day and night—these are the "M&M's" of knowing Jesus and developing a true Jesus heart.

The greatest journey of my life began in 1974 at a Bill Gothard conference in Tulsa, Oklahoma. I don't remember many things the lecturer said, but I will never forget his exhortation to memorize and meditate on God's Word chapter by chapter, book by book.

When I read the criteria for Attention Deficit Hyperactivity Disorder (ADHD), I get an almost perfect score. I was born distracted! On top of that, I played defensive line at SMU and coached the defensive line at Texas A&M. Nothing against football guys, but we nose tackles are not generally famous for deep academic endeavors and are not often displayed on bronze plaques down the hallways of summa cum laude.

Memorizing and *meditating* were two words that might as well have been from Mars. I was clueless on where to begin and how to concentrate long enough to get it done. Yet I walked away from that Gothard conference convinced and committed to begin a new chapter in my walk with Jesus.

I stuck my nose into three memory courses for an insightful beginning. They all said the same thing: "You can't memorize words, but you can't forget pictures." To be able to *meditate* on God's Word, you have to first *memorize* it. Though the nuances vary from one memory expert to another, they all seem to have that one fact in common: Memorizing words is frustrating, but memorizing pictures is fun!

You, too, can become an avid "M&M fan" with the following tried-and-true practices:

1. Set a goal with a certain passage of Scripture, a start date, and a completion date.

2. Get a friend involved to provide accountability.

3. Give yourself a reward at the completion of the goal. For example, when my children were 10, I told them I'd get them a used car when they turned 16 if they would memorize the books of 2 Timothy and Philippians with me. Three of my kids completed the task. One of them also memorized the book of James as a surprise Christmas present (the best Christmas gift I ever received)!

4. Put the words you're memorizing into pictures; the more vivid the picture, the better. For example, the word *believe* is a picture of a "bee leaving" a place. The term *He who* is a picture of an owl with a football helmet on his head. (That makes him a *he who*!)

5. Every night before bed, when you wake up at night, when you wake up in the morning, when you're driving, when you're traveling by air, and when you're exercising or having an idle moment, repeat over in your mind what you've been memorizing.

For greater intimacy with Jesus, I like meditating on some of David's more affectionate psalms like 16, 34, 51, 91, 100, 103, and 145.

I also find myself abiding with Him more closely when I meditate on His conversation in John 13–16 and Matthew 5–7. Paul's, Peter's, and John's letters have also been monumental in my quest to know Jesus more deeply and fully.

One night, I called home from Nashville, Tennessee,

where I was recruiting staff for our sports camps, to check in on my bride and kids. My wife was chuckling when she answered the phone. "What's so funny?" I asked.

She told me about the bedside conversation she had just enjoyed with our younger son, Cooper, who was five at that time and still sucking his thumb. As she tucked him in bed and told him good night, he pulled his thumb out of his mouth and said, "Mom, I want to memorize another Bible verse tonight, so when Dad comes home I can tell it to him."

My wife responded in typical Debbie-Jo candor, "Children obey your parents, for this is pleasing to God."

Cooper pulled his thumb out of his mouth again and said, "That's not in there!"

Debbie-Jo said, "Yes it is, Cooper."

He quickly responded, "That's not in there, you just made that up!"

Pick any chapter or book you want and begin this thrilling adventure as soon as you can. It's all in there. Nobody "just made that up"!

When you finish memorizing a chapter, go treat yourself to a thick, creamy chocolate milkshake at your favorite In-N-Out Burger or Chick-fil-A. I know from experience that you'll never enjoy anything as much in your life. (I'm talking about the memorization, not the milkshake.)

After Michael Phelps won eight gold medals in the 2008 Olympics in Beijing, the swimming world stood in awe of the new icon. He had just broken the seemingly unconquerable record of Mark Spitz, who had won seven at the Munich Olympics in 1972.

With the world as his stage, Phelps unmasked the simple secret of gold-medal thinking in every aspect of life: "If you want to succeed, do things other people are unwilling to do."

Almost every high-school football player, at some point in his career, dreams of playing in the NFL. Yet only one out of every 1,000 gets to see his dream come true.

Only four out of every 10,000 male high-school basketball players ends up playing in the NBA.

Only five out of every 1,000 high-school baseball players ends up playing Major League Baseball.

Every sincere believer longs for a deep relationship with Jesus, yet so few really go there.

Meditating on Scripture day and night for the sole purpose of knowing Jesus with remarkable peace and intimacy is the simple scriptural mandate. But I meet precious few who are willing to work joyfully and relentlessly to "go deep" in this fantastic life adventure.

I hear the same excuses, like a broken record, for why men and women, from adolescence to the retirement home, don't pursue Jesus' heart on scriptural meditation as expressed in His Word.

"I'm not good at memory work."

"I've tried before and it just doesn't work for me."

"I'm way too ADHD for that."

"I just like to open the Bible and let it open to wherever God leads me."

"Memorization is just not my bag."

I can hear the adversary laughing from the portals of hell.

Perhaps you've thought the same things and have let Satan's voice of defeat rule your thinking and steal Jesus' intimacy from your faith experience. That was me, too!

My "absentmindedness" that plagued me from birth made memory work daunting. Twice, I've been talking on my cell phone to one of my children, and I remarked, "Oh, man, I've lost my cell phone again. Why can't I keep up with that thing?"

"Dad," they said with a chuckle, "look in your left hand!"

If you want a bronze medal in a race, train like everybody else. If you want the gold, set your mind on gold, and go get it.

Wilma Rudolph, the great sprinter who won three gold medals in the 1960 Rome Olympics, was running one chilly early morning through a quiet neighborhood. Someone asked, "Why aren't you home sleeping like everyone else?"

The famous Olympian remarked, "They're not going where I'm going."

Ready to be drawn into Jesus' irresistible love? Stop reading the Bible and *treasure* it. Stop going to the Word; *run* to it. Stop working at it and *delight* in it.

Run from measured quiet times and "scorekeeping" studies! Paul did not say, "That I might know *about* Him." In the Philippian letter, rather, he cried out, "That I might know Him!" (Philippians 3:10).

Precepts, Bible Study Fellowship, and church-based programs are brilliant! But like a Kentucky Derby racehorse, the thoroughbred that *loves* to run and possesses the desire to win will get the blue ribbon every time.

Like a good pitcher of Southern sun tea, put the bag in the water and let it steep for a few hours out in the sunshine. Let it brew slowly. Think deeply about the words as the verse, chapter, and book become part of your life. Meditate on them when you're on the treadmill, when you're driving home from the kids' soccer practice, when you're sitting in class (while everyone else is checking their Instagram), when you're waiting in the doctor's office, or when you're waiting for your business contact to pick up the phone.

Fill the countless gaps, big and small, with a heavenly addiction. Turn Facebook time into "His Book" time.

Fall in love with Jesus' Word. Go for gold!

"I shall delight in Your commandments, which I love. And I shall lift up my hands to Your commandments, which I love; and I will meditate on Your statutes. . . . Your statutes are my songs in the house of my pilgrimage. . . . The law of Your mouth is better to me than thousands of gold and silver pieces" (Psalm 119:47-48, 54, 72).

My 16-year-old younger son had just won an exhilarating seven-on-seven summer league football game as a quarterback. He was ecstatic. On the way to the used car lot for his first driving experience, he recited Philippians and 2 Timothy to me one last time. We had spent the better part of four years, during "lay by times," memorizing and meditating on those two books. (He wanted to do Titus and Philemon!)

That night, he came to my bedroom with a tender smile on his face (man, can that kid smile) and said, "Dad, thanks for the keys. But more than that, thanks for taking so much time to memorize Scripture with me."

"Why do you say that?" I answered in shock.

"Because someday that car will die, but the Bible will be with me forever."

"How can a young man keep his way pure? By keeping it according to Your word. With all my heart I have sought You; do not let me wander from Your commandments. Your word I have treasured in my heart, that I may not sin against You" (Psalm 119:9-11).

PERSEVERANCE PAYS

For 35 years, a woman named Mary prayed for her husband. For 35 years, he rebuffed her. When Mary and Marvin's two children came to our summer camps, they trusted Christ and returned to share their newly found faith with their dad.

"Hogwash," he responded. "It's all hogwash."

The two young believers were not deterred. They joined their mom in prayer for him.

Mary's mom died in early October. A week later, Marvin died, Shortly thereafter, Mary and I connected on an unforgettable phone call. "How are you, Mary?" I asked. "I can't imagine how difficult this must have been for you."

To my pleasant surprise, Mary was upbeat and joyful. "I'm living off a memory," she responded. "The kids and I witnessed a miracle."

"Tell me about it, Mary," I pressed.

Mary proceeded to tell me the story of her countless prayers and attempts to lead Marvin out of his dark stubbornness. She told me about her graceful persistence in prayer.

"Just before Marvin died," she continued, "as he lay quietly in bed, slowly breathing his last few breaths, I looked into his face and said, 'Marvin, may I tell you about Jesus one last time?'"

She said he fixed his eyes on her lips and granted her request.

One final round before the closing bell, Mary shared God's plan of salvation and eternal life through His Son's sacrificial death on the cross. Before Marvin took his final breath and closed his eyes for his eternal judgment, he whispered these two words to his faithful, praying wife, "I believe."

In Luke 18:1-8, Jesus clearly exhorted believers to be like

Mary and her children and never stop praying. Hear the words of His parable:

> Now He was telling them a parable to show that at all times they ought to pray and not to lose heart, saying, "In a certain city there was a judge who did not fear God and did not respect man. There was a widow in that city, and she kept coming to him, saying, 'Give me legal protection from my opponent.' For a while he was unwilling; but afterward he said to himself, 'Even though I do not fear God nor respect man, yet because this widow bothers me, I will give her legal protection, otherwise by continually coming she will wear me out.'" And the Lord said, "Hear what the unrighteous judge said; now, will not God bring about justice for His elect who cry to Him day and night, and will He delay long over them? I tell you that He will bring about justice for them quickly. However, when the Son of Man comes, will He find faith on the earth?"

First Thessalonians 5:17 gives a seemingly impossible directive when Paul scripturally proclaimed, "Pray without ceasing."

To an ADHD brain like mine that struggles constantly to focus on any sustaining thought, the exhortation seems daunting, to say the least. Even though I still feel as if it's my first day in kindergarten, trying to color within the lines of the coloring book of prayerful silhouettes, Scripture memorization and meditation have been my meager offering of hope.

To memorize a chapter or book in the Word of God by taking a verse of Scripture a day, a chapter a semester, or any reasonable goal requires consistent attention to meet the established mark. Because of the powerful psychological process of cognition, when scriptural memory goals are established, God's Word maintains its presence in your mind throughout the day and night.

One of Jesus' most astounding promises is found in Hebrews 4:16 when He said, through the author's pen, "Therefore let us draw near with confidence to the throne of grace, so that we may receive mercy and find grace to help in time of need."

If there is anything on earth more wonderful than that truth, I have no idea what it could possibly be.

DRAWING CLOSE IN PRAYER

Picture the Temple of God in ancient Jerusalem. Carefully established by King Solomon in the tenth century BC, it contained the Holy of Holies, where God could be encountered only once a year by the high priest—and only after he had undergone an exhaustive series of sacrifices and cleansing. Here in this sanctified room, the high priest could come to the mercy seat of God with fear and trembling, carrying the sins of his nation to the listening ear of the merciful Creator.

In the crucifixion account, Scripture explains that upon Jesus' death, the veil closing off this most holy room was torn in half, granting all sincere believers access to the mercy seat. Hebrews 10:20-22 explains God's purpose in that historical moment and His greatest invitation to believers who seek His face in prayer: "By a new and living way which He inaugurated for us through the veil, that is, His flesh, and since we have a great priest over the house of God, let us draw near with a sincere heart in full assurance of faith, having our hearts sprinkled clean from an evil conscience and our bodies washed with pure water."

What a magnificent promise! What an offering of God's grace! What an invitation to conversation with Jesus!

Praying Scripture in a personal context is the great key to intimacy with Jesus. You may want to employ the ACTS plan that has been super helpful in keeping my distracted mind on track:

Adoration: memorize and meditate on Psalm 145.
Confession: memorize and meditate on Psalm 51.
Thanksgiving: memorize and meditate on Psalm 100.
Supplication: memorize and meditate on Philippians 4:5-7.

Scriptural prayer changes things.
Scriptural prayer builds relationships.
Scriptural prayer brings healing and forgiveness.
Scriptural prayer makes going to sleep at night a peaceful experience.
Scriptural prayer makes waking up in the morning a hopeful experience.
Scriptural prayer makes waking up in the middle of the night a pleasant experience.
Scriptural prayer brings a family together in an inseparable bond.

The highlight of my day and the best daily event in my four decades of marriage to Debbie-Jo is so simple. Before we say our final "good nights," I simply take her hand and ask, "Baby, how can I pray for you tonight?" She then shares a few thoughts, and I pray them out loud.

It is crazy how simple, how brief, and yet how profound that can be.

8

CHOOSING JOY

As we make our journey through life with the Lord, some-times it's hard to remember the last word in Philippians 4:4 —"Rejoice in the Lord always." We are to rejoice *always*, in all situations, knowing that God's irresistible love will never leave us. There have been certain people and events in my life to remind me of this truth. Let me share them with you.

+ + +

When I put on my old, brown round-toed cowboy boots each morning, I feel like I'm getting a hug from a longtime friend. I wear them to archery hunt, to work outside, to the office, and to speak at conferences. Their job one smiley-faced day a few years back was to take me to an event at the University of Southern California.

I'll never forget my flight layover in Dallas. Of all America's airports, DFW is my favorite. Besides offering any type of Dallas Cowboy T-shirt you've ever imagined, there are a number of Texas barbeque shops, Texas praline candy outlets, shiny Texas cowboy boot stores, and stores that sell gaudy Texas silver belt buckles, Texas flags, and even Texas cactus jelly for the extreme loyalists.

Between flights, I had a 90-minute layover, so I did a little window shopping and reminisced about my Texas childhood and SMU football.

I looked down at my dirty, beat-up boots, and it dawned on me that the minute I landed at my next destination, I'd be whisked off to an event facing a crowd of highly expectant West Coast college students. Looking like an Ozark Mountain hillbilly probably wouldn't meet their expectations of an event speaker. Fortunately, just down the corridor from my connecting gate was a shoeshine stand. An open seat on the platform presented itself, so I asked the dear gentleman attending it for a shine.

His smile, his laughter, and his entire countenance reflected B.J. Thomas's old favorite hit song *Happy Man* to the letter.

As the man and I struck up a friendship, he told me his personal story filled with a constant barrage of trials and tragedies. He told me of his wife of 21 years who fought cancer and of his daughter who had a disability. He talked of being laid off from his job, but his smile never dimmed as he relived his tale. He still had faith in God. "I get up each day with a positive attitude," he said with a grin. He'd probably shared his story with others a thousand times.

In 15 minutes, that man took a pair of boots that looked as if Indiana Jones had worn them on a jungle trek and turned them into a pair of "spit-shined" gems.

I was so inspired by the man and his "joy of the Lord."

CHOICES

After I was diagnosed with leukemia, I had to undergo the occasional bone marrow extraction for the purpose of pinpoint accuracy in diagnosis and subsequent treatments. Dr. Robert Johnson, my oncologist from Memphis, Tennessee, was the first doctor to perform these procedures on my lower back.

I have to confess I was a little nervous going into the first extraction. The thought of someone drilling into my backbone under only local anesthetic didn't exactly sound like a Sunday afternoon picnic. For some reason, he had to try three times to retrieve the first successful specimen. So I went to the local Walmart and purchased a dart board and a half dozen throw darts for the good doctor and presented them to him with special instructions that he practice diligently before the next procedure.

In the 13 major surgeries and who knows how many biopsies and "minor surgeries and afflictions" I've been blessed to live through in my adult life, I have found there's no greater place for an all-out party than a hospital room before and after surgery. Doctors, nurses, orderlies, and anesthesiologists don't even need invitations. They're guaranteed to show up!

There are "praisers" and there are "groaners," as my good friend Ken Poure used to say. Life is full of surprises. Jesus even promised in His last speech before His crucifixion, "In the world you have tribulation, but take courage; I have overcome the world" (John 16:33).

But having fun is a choice. "No bad days" is a decision.

I'm 100 percent positive that Romans 8:28 was written to let us know He *always* has a fantastic plan for the most difficult days ahead. It reads, "And we know that God causes all things to work together for good to those who love God, to those who are called according to His purpose."

My dad used to say, "Growing older isn't for cowards." At my stage in life, all the moving parts of this machine God "fearfully and wonderfully made" to carry this old bag of bones around in has somehow outlasted the manufacturer's warranty. You can bet your bottom dollar it will run out for you as well.

You can either laugh at life or life will laugh at you.

When I look at Jesus in His final triumphant hours and see "the joy that was set before Him" sparkling in those blood-filled eyes, I am positive I can do the same in the "momentary light afflictions" I'm asked to endure. As I sit here writing today, eating my favorite candy bar, the luscious Peter Paul Almond Joy, I feel fairly qualified to say that joy, love, and laughter in the midst of life's many "curveballs" are some ways, if not *the greatest* ways, to fall deeply in love with the One who did it best.

A TRUE HERO

One of my true heroes was a 16-year-old, blue-eyed girl from Reed Springs, Missouri, named Lori Anne Hagerman. I first met Lori Anne at one of our exuberant K-Life clubs in Branson, Missouri, where 80 or so wild high school students would gather at "7:14½ p.m." each Sunday night. The kids were almost as rowdy as their leader! I knew that having fun with kids was the greatest way to get them off the street and into a relationship with Jesus.

I particularly noticed Lori Anne one Sunday evening because of the black patch covering one of her eyes. I asked one of our leaders who she was. The leader told me her name and said she had just returned from surgery, where the doctor had found a cancerous tumor in her eye that had to be removed.

I began to draw close to this precious young girl with one dazzling blue eye and a heart bigger than her petite frame. As Lori Anne's and my relationship grew, so did her relationship with Jesus. She was so close to Him in those days and reflected His love, joy, and peace so clearly that she drew not only me but also her friends into a deeper relationship with her Savior.

Over the next two years, Lori Anne's tumors in her face grew and brought her incredible pain. As her life came to a close at the MD Anderson Cancer Center in Houston, Texas, three or four of her doctors gathered around her bed to tell her the cancer drugs were not working and she needed to prepare herself to die.

Nevertheless, Lori Anne continued to bring a blessing to everyone who approached her. As I would visit her, hoping to bring a word of peace and joy, it was I who received the greatest blessing. So also it was with the doctors who treated her. She squinted her one remaining eye and said, "Don't worry about your medicine running out. I won't die when your medicine quits working. I will die when my Jesus calls me home."

She returned to our local Branson hospital for her final week to be close to her family. I remember grieving as I heard the sad news of her imminent departure.

A few days before Lori Anne died, a teenage pop star was playing a concert in a nearby city. I went there to ask him to come down and meet Lori Anne. I found my way into his dressing room after the show and told him about the young girl who was dying in the hospital just 35 miles away. He asked me to pick him up the next morning. Coincidentally, that night Lori Anne was watching TV, and he had made an appearance on the show she was viewing.

The next morning, he sang to her and kissed her before I took him back to his tour bus for the trip to his next gig.

Two days later, a priest was visiting Lori Anne, and he exclaimed, "I hear a rock star visited your room!"

Lori Anne responded with her typical candor, "What's a rock star when you're going to meet Jesus in a week?"

As painful as the countless tumors in her face undoubtedly were, piggybacked with the sorrow of saying good-bye to her friends and family at such a young age, Lori Anne was still able to smile, laugh, and "for the joy set before her" find a way to make others smile even unto her last, beautiful breath.

Perhaps that's why Paul could rejoice in the Lord even after the many ordeals he endured and described in 2 Corinthians 11:23-28:

> . . . in far more labors, in far more imprisonments, beaten times without number, often in danger of death. Five times I received from the Jews thirty-nine lashes. Three times I was beaten with rods, once I was stoned, three times I was shipwrecked, a night and a day I have spent in the deep. I have been on frequent journeys, in dangers from rivers, dangers from robbers, dangers from my countrymen, dangers from the Gentiles, dangers in the city, dangers in the wilderness, dangers on the sea, dangers among false brethren; I have been in labor and hardship, through many sleepless nights, in hunger and thirst, often without food, in cold and exposure. Apart from such external things, there is the daily pressure on me of concern for all the churches.

Rejoicing in the Lord always was Paul's theme song, the genesis of his joy. Even in his treacherous imprisonment, it was his mind-set to be thankful in all things (see 1 Thessalonians 5:18).

You see, intimate love is conceived in the womb of thanksgiving. Thanksgiving is conceived in the womb of joy. Joy is conceived in wisdom. Wisdom is conceived in knowledge. Knowledge is conceived in the Word. And, completing the circle, the Word is conceived in the heart of the Savior whose irresistible love gives us reason for joy.

9

KNOWING GOD
THROUGH TRIALS

LEUKEMIA. Film and TV screenplay writers have used the word countless times to draw a tear from a captivated audience. I'm a sucker for those kinds of writers. I'm the first to cry and the last to leave the theater at the end of the movie. There's one thing all "leukemia dramas" have in common: the main character always dies.

I had experienced only one personal leukemia story, with a dear Latino friend. His name was Dr. Roberto Olivares, and he was from Sherman, Texas. "Dr. O" was a splendid fellow. As a dad and husband, he was pure excellence. His five children—Rocquel, Rosalyn, Ricky, Rebecca, and Roberto—adored him.

He would have been a world-class grandpa, adored and known as Santa Claus. His days, however, ended painfully before his dreams of being a granddad began. I watched that dear man suffer and then lose a 20-year battle with leukemia. He died as he lived, with pure class.

The last time I visited the brilliant urologist, he was lying on his deathbed, fighting the pain of disease and the pain of saying good-bye. I walked into his hospital room to give him one last hug. His eyes opened to half-mast, and a grin sheepishly crept across his face as he tried to masquerade his intense pain. "Joe," he whispered, "God is so good. He is so very, very good."

Then he smiled as he looked at his charming wife of four decades and said in his broken accent, "Look at her. Isn't she beautiful?"

Even to gently touch his skin sent shooting pain throughout his body. Great relief prevailed in the Olivares family prayer camp when he finally closed his eyes and breathed his last breath.

You never think it will happen to you.

THE DIAGNOSIS

I was 50 years old the summer my younger son began serious training to prepare his athletic body for college football. He approached me in early June to give me one of the favorite blessings of my lifetime. "Hey, Dad," he asked, "will you train me and get me ready for college football?"

I had coached high-school and college football. I had trained several thousand athletes at both levels at our sports camps over the previous 25 years. But being invited to coach my son was the greatest moment of my coaching life.

Late in the summer, as Cooper and I ran sprints together, I noticed large, hard bruises emerging on my legs. I never bruised much playing football, so it was easy to tell that my capillary system was breaking down and a disease was erupting inside my body.

The last week of our training, I slipped off to a local hospital for a blood exam. A few days later, as Cooper and I wrapped up our final workout, the volunteer camp doctor approached me on the football field with the results of my blood test gripped in his hand. His name was Buddy Rawlings, and he just happened to be an oncologist who specialized in blood cancer. As he approached me, he appeared solemn and deeply pensive. His face looked as if he had just returned from a funeral. He asked me to walk down and sit in his car with him.

He stammered through his proclamation. "Joe," he muttered, "there are two words a person fears the most, *cancer* and *leukemia*. You've got both!" He explained that the only cure was a bone marrow transplant. At age 50, my chance of survival was slim, and if I did survive, I'd never be the same person as before.

His words hit me like a truckload of bricks in the center of my gut. I was stunned. I looked at the giant bruises on my hamstrings that reinforced the message that I was dying, literally bleeding to death inside my skin. My white blood count was 30 times more than normal. My systems would soon go into shock.

I left Dr. Rawlings's car and raced for Cooper. He was packing his car for his trip to college. I threw my arms around his neck and wept as I told him the report.

He pushed back in disbelief and asked me the most difficult question I've ever been confronted with: "Dad, have you told Mom?"

The thought of telling my bride was horrifying. She had

already lost her dad and stepdad, and now would I abandon her too?

"Dad, you've got to tell Mom," Cooper insisted.

I staggered over to our little cabin where we lived while directing the teenage sports camp from mid-May to early August. Debbie-Jo was there. My face told the story before I could get the words out of my mouth.

"What's wrong, honey?" she asked.

"Baby, I'm sick. Doc says I'm not doing well. It . . . it doesn't look good. I've got leukemia."

The next two days were horrible. Three of my children were nearby. Sharing the prognosis with each one was indescribably difficult, but I couldn't talk about it at the Christian camp my wife and I operate because my younger daughter was in graduate school in Seattle, and I couldn't let her hear about it from others. I had to see her and talk through it face-to-face. She was in a fragile time in her own life. We had been super close throughout her childhood, and I was her pillar during some difficult years. She was my little champion; I was her leaning post.

As I drove out of the camp we had built 30 years prior, I said good-bye, thinking I'd probably never return. I had put my all into that beautiful place and watched God revolutionize adolescents' lives. Saying good-bye was awful.

The trip to Seattle was long and lonely. I feared my daughter's reaction to the news. I wept as I took her into my arms and explained my illness. The night was dreadful for both of us. Saying good-bye to those you've poured your life into is heartwrenching. This girl and I had walked through some long, difficult valleys together. My love for her was like a storybook.

After I returned home, my wife and I traveled to the

famed Mayo Clinic in Rochester, Minnesota. The team of brilliant doctors extracted my bone marrow and blood and began the series of lab tests. Confirming the diagnosis, a magnificent doctor from Ethiopia reiterated what the camp doctor and a cancer specialist from Memphis, Tennessee, named Dr. Robert Johnson had said a few days before. My chances of survival with or without treatment weren't good. "Mr. White, you need to go home and get your house in order," the Mayo doctor said.

"However," he cautiously continued, "a genetic research team at Washington State University has been developing a brand-new experimental drug that could possibly be a remedy." If I were willing and could qualify for the test group, perhaps I would have a chance.

I had an encounter with God that night in the Rochester hotel room that was truly the most intimate experience of my life. Jesus showed Himself to me in a precious, tender vision as a tender, nurturing dad! The picture He gave me was myself as a little boy on my hands and knees on the five-yard line of the football field I'd been running down my whole life. I saw myself knocked to the ground and bleeding in pain. I saw the end zone ahead of me as if it were eternity; I saw the end zone as heaven. I couldn't get in by myself. I couldn't cross the goal line and score.

I looked up into the darkness as I knelt on the floor in that hotel room and asked as I wept profusely, "God, will You be there? Will You be there at the end?" In that picture in my mind, He scooped me up in His arms and placed my head on His chest. He carried me lovingly across the goal line and told me three times, "I will carry you at the end. I will carry you across the goal line. I will carry you in at the end of the race."

How God gave that dear research team the nontoxic macromolecular formula for the cure for the specific strain of CML leukemia that had stricken my body at that exact time in history, I'll never know until I get to heaven and see the entire miraculous picture.

"For now we see in a mirror dimly, but then face to face; now I know in part, but then I will know fully just as I also have been fully known" (1 Corinthians 13:12).

THE JOURNEY

By the grace of God, I was placed in the test group and began to receive the drug. The daily dose of STI571 was instantly effective.

The next five years were tentative, gratefully tearful at times, and inexplicably tender. Holding hands with my wife as we prayed together each night before bed was incredibly intimate. I was speaking at 30 to 40 events each year on college campuses and in sport arenas packed with men. As I shared the drama of the crucifixion of Jesus, thousands of individuals would parade out of their seats to place their faith in Him. I was tearfully hugging as many of them as I could get to. At NFL and college team events, on several occasions, the whole team would come up for a reassuring "daddy hug."

God was using my affliction to draw me close to students and men who suffered from their own afflictions. You could say His irresistible love for me was becoming my relentless love for them.

Several Bible verses that I was meditating on in those ever-so-tender days were coming alive before my eyes:

"[He] comforts us in all our affliction so that we will be able to comfort those who are in any affliction with the comfort with which we ourselves are comforted by God"

(2 Corinthians 1:4). I was amazed, night after night, how truly astounding it was to see that promise come to life.

"Most gladly, therefore, I will rather boast about my weaknesses, so that the power of Christ may dwell in me" (2 Corinthians 12:9).

"[We are] always carrying about in the body the dying of Jesus, so that the life of Jesus also may be manifested in our body" (2 Corinthians 4:10).

I had *never* seen God work so personally in my life. It was as if I were just a spectator as I delivered the drama at the cross and watched God miraculously bring His lost sheep back to the fold and adopt them into His family of faith.

No one knew, however, how long this test drug would last. Reports on the internet said some patients had developed a resistance to the drug and relapsed. My emotions escalated and crashed like a roller coaster—from the euphoria of seeing thousands surrender their lives to Jesus at the events to the reality of the uncertain length of my days with my wife and children.

"For to me, to live is Christ and to die is gain" (Philippians 1:21).

In my early days with leukemia, on a Friday afternoon in mid-July, a watershed moment occurred as I showered to get ready to travel to Providence, Rhode Island, for a Promise Keepers event. Although I've never heard the audible voice of God, I clearly heard His voice in the quietness of my heart that day.

I believe it was His "still, quiet voice" that said, "Joe, would you give Me the remaining 30 years of your life if one man got saved tonight?"

In my self-first reaction, I responded, "I don't know." Thoughts of saying good-bye to my bride, my children, and my grandchildren flashed through my mind. It was ever-so-deeply troubling to my spirit.

I stepped out of the shower, dried off, and dressed. As I grabbed the handle of my black travel bag, God showed me a picture of that saved man in heaven after a trillion years. I didn't see his face, but I clearly saw God's intended message.

I froze in my tracks. I paused and apologized. "Yes, God," I said. "If my cancer could relate to that man with the 'cancer' of porn or bitterness or rejection, and my cancer would cost me my life, I'd definitely exchange my remaining 30 years for his eternity. In a trillion years," I added, "who will care if I lived to 50 or to 80?"

God's reassuring comfort of fatherly love at that moment was worth everything. He was real, and He was close.

That evening in Providence was one of my favorite times of my life. At the end of the cross drama, 6,000 men got up out of their seats to come forward to exchange their old lives for a new life in Christ. The conversation in the shower and the experience in Providence with those humble, broken men were as fondly unforgettable as life this side of heaven can be.

Since those affectionate days with God have passed, 2 Corinthians 4:11 has become a treasure to me: "For we who live are constantly being delivered over to death for Jesus' sake, so that the life of Jesus also may be manifested in our mortal flesh."

What I didn't know then was that deeper and greater opportunity for God's promise, "my death for his life," waited just around the corner.

SAINT JOHN OF THE CROSS

My next dark period arrived with the discovery of prostate cancer. Two years of dark depression followed due to an accumulation of pressures in my life. As a result, I could at least scratch the surface of Saint John of the Cross's expression of his pilgrimage through brokenness in *The Dark Night of the Soul.*[1]

In his cherished work, Juan de Yepes (Saint John of the Cross) revealed, through his compelling poetry, his personal understanding of utter poverty, solitary confinement, torturous floggings, and endless lack of comfort through the bitter cold of winter and the blistering heat of summer.

Saint John of the Cross wrote, "Why, since you wounded this heart, don't you heal it? And why, since you stole it from me, do you leave it so, and fail to carry off what you have stolen? Extinguish these miseries, since no one else can stamp them out; and may my eyes behold you, because you are their light, and I would open them to you alone. Reveal your presence, and may the vision of your beauty be my death; for the sickness of love is not cured except by your very presence and image."[2]

In life's darkest trials, this expression hits the bull's-eye perfectly.

Tom Bowen is, to me, a modern version of Saint John of the Cross. I first met Tom at a men's event in Memphis, Tennessee, where I was to speak. The event leaders wanted me to encounter this remarkable New York City fire and rescue professional who had been severely injured in his post-9/11 duty of locating and removing the deceased from the ruins of the World Trade Center.

Tom was temporarily living at St. Jude Children's Research Hospital in Memphis, where his two-year-old son, Ben, was receiving surgical treatments and chemotherapeutics for a severe brain tumor called AT/RT.

Tom's positive countenance reminded me of an oft-quoted

but seldom-experienced-in-modern-American-life Scripture: "In this you greatly rejoice, even though now for a little while, if necessary, you have been distressed by various trials, so that the proof of your faith, being more precious than gold which is perishable, even though tested by fire, may be found to result in praise and glory and honor at the revelation of Jesus Christ" (1 Peter 1:6-7).

Even though Tom was suffering from personal injuries and the emotional trauma of enduring his son's agonizing medical afflictions, his faith, graciousness, and confidence in the Lord struck me to the core of my being. As I beheld his beautiful, bald-headed son with surgical scars running down the length and width of his skull, I was moved into deep, empathetic remorse.

The way Tom carried himself emotionally and spiritually was inspirational beyond description.

Tom gave me a long section of a fire hose used in the 9/11 firefight and explained to me "The Lifeline Principle" that is understood by firefighters throughout the world. "The four-inch-diameter fire hose," he said, "especially in the case of a tall burning building, is the only pathway out of the blazing furnace. As each firefighter battles the heat, smoke, and falling debris, he *must* keep one hand on 'the lifeline' or he will surely get lost in the confusion and perish in the building." Tom's story became the theme of my emotional address to the men of the conference.

After my unforgettable introduction to this impressive warrior, Ben's condition deteriorated into months of agonizing pain. It's true that the greatest pain inflicted on an adult is the pain of a suffering child. In the last, harrowing weeks of Ben's life, he ground his teeth down to the gum line while writhing in pain. To touch the lad would set his body on fire.

After helplessly watching his son suffer and die, Tom's own condition worsened. While he was being resuscitated from his injurious fall into the World Trade Center wreckage, his breathing apparatus filled with contaminants, which entered his lungs and caused damaging lesions. Tom would face surgery after surgery to remove a portion of his lung and several adjacent lesions. His surgeries enabled him to cling to life and continue to parent his other children.

To my pleasant surprise, Tom reconnected with me one recent night and told me, as Paul Harvey used to say, "the rest of the story." Tom wasn't bitter. He wasn't angry. He didn't harbor the least sense of disdain toward God.

In sheer amazement I asked my dear friend, "How do you keep the faith?"

Tom calmly explained how, in spite of his continuous raging nightmares, endless pain, and sleeplessness, his light never dims, his faith never wanes, and his love for his Savior is never diminished.

"How, Tom, how?" I questioned. "How do you hold on? How do you *go* on?"

He said his healing had come through countless hours of worshiping God through music and meditating on Scripture. Even though he still suffers from nighttime panic attacks where he pictures his children in the pits and ashes of the World Trade Center rubble, his faith carries him like a mom cuddling her newborn baby. "But the greatest faith sustainer," he said, "is that I realize and exercise God's great purpose for it all."

"We know that God causes all things to work together for

good to those who love God, to those who are called according to His purpose" (Romans 8:28).

He explained how his son's heroic fight had been a great encouragement to all the staff, parents, and patients at Saint Jude's, as well as the tens of thousands who followed Tom's blog detailing Ben's journey and fight for survival.

Tom continued to unfold his personal pilgrimage as a minister to countless soldiers who returned from the battlefields in the Middle East with post-traumatic stress disorder. They swarm to him as bees swarm to honey.

Tom believes the promise of 2 Corinthians 1:4 is written for him, and he clutches that promise with all the strength he has left: "[He] comforts us in all our affliction so that we will be able to comfort those who are in any affliction with the comfort with which we ourselves are comforted by God."

Tom tenderly but confidently adds, "My tears represent my yielding to Him. I don't have to be the one who figures it out. When I weep, it reminds me I can't make it on my own. When I worship, I can't even utter the words to the songs. They are so humbling and breaking."

Tom says of his divinely inspired purpose to walk alongside our military servicemen who return from battle in mental torment, "I get to place the journey of Christ in me into them. My journey becomes their journey. Before I was able to minister to them, they were checked out, but since I've been there before, our relationships explode, and they often become purpose-driven guys."

Tom attributes his hope and deep sense of purpose to Jesus on the cross. "His call in 1 Peter 2:21-24 gives me hope. I believe in God's promises. Jesus has gone before me. He understands my suffering."

You have been called for this purpose, since Christ
also suffered for you, leaving you an example for you
to follow in His steps, who committed no sin, nor
was any deceit found in His mouth; and while being
reviled, He did not revile in return; while suffering,
He uttered no threats, but kept entrusting Himself
to Him who judges righteously; and He Himself
bore our sins in His body on the cross, so that we
might die to sin and live to righteousness; for by His
wounds you were healed.

1 PETER 2:21-24

Prophetically, 1,000 years before Jesus was born and 800
years before the Assyrians invented the cruelty of human
crucifixion, David prophesied Jesus' experience of suffering
and death in verses 1, 2, and 14-18 of Psalm 22:

My God, my God, why have You forsaken me?
Far from my deliverance are the words of my groaning.
O my God, I cry by day, but You do not answer;
And by night, but I have no rest. . . .
I am poured out like water,
And all my bones are out of joint;
My heart is like wax;
It is melted within me.
My strength is dried up like a potsherd,
And my tongue cleaves to my jaws;
And You lay me in the dust of death.
For dogs have surrounded me;
A band of evildoers has encompassed me;
They pierced my hands and my feet.
I can count all my bones.

They look, they stare at me;
They divide my garments among them,
And for my clothing they cast lots.

The fellowship of suffering that David, Peter, and Paul experienced not only carried them through their days of intense affliction, but like Tom, it also allowed them to cherish the pain as they were drawn so tenderly, so intimately, and so soulfully close to the One who'd been there before.

But whatever things were gain to me, those things
I have counted as loss for the sake of Christ. More
than that, I count all things to be loss in view of the
surpassing value of knowing Christ Jesus my Lord, for
whom I have suffered the loss of all things, and count
them but rubbish so that I may gain Christ, and may
be found in Him, not having a righteousness of my
own derived from the Law, but that which is through
faith in Christ, the righteousness which comes from
God on the basis of faith, that I may know Him and
the power of His resurrection and the fellowship of
His sufferings, being conformed to His death; in order
that I may attain to the resurrection from the dead.
    Not that I have already obtained it, or have
already become perfect, but I press on so that I may
lay hold of that for which also I was laid hold of
by Christ Jesus. Brethren, I do not regard myself
as having laid hold of it yet; but one thing I do:
forgetting what lies behind and reaching forward to
what lies ahead, I press on toward the goal for the
prize of the upward call of God in Christ Jesus.

PHILIPPIANS 3:7-14

And He has said to me, "My grace is sufficient for you, for power is perfected in weakness." Most gladly, therefore, I will rather boast about my weaknesses, so that the power of Christ may dwell in me. Therefore I am well content with weaknesses, with insults, with distresses, with persecutions, with difficulties, for Christ's sake; for when I am weak, then I am strong.

2 CORINTHIANS 12:9-10

I am weary with my sighing; every night I make my bed swim, I dissolve my couch with my tears. My eye has wasted away with grief; it has become old because of all my adversaries.

PSALM 6:6-7

For Tom Bowen and me, it was during those days when the thick, dark cloud of sadness stubbornly loomed over our heads that we met "the God I never knew."

YOUR OWN VALLEY

Perhaps you've walked "through the valley of the shadow of death" as well. Perhaps you're trodding through that valley today, or perhaps those days are ahead. Rest assured that God is faithful to His promises, and in the times of greatest despair, four divine providences will always be yours in Christ.

First, He will give you, as He has given me, 20/20 vision looking backward to see His hand in everything. The future may look uncertain, and the current conditions may feel too dark to muster the courage to continue, but the dark cloud is not a stationary object. As the skies begin to clear, you'll find Him walking alongside you and directing the affairs of your life like the conductor of a symphony orchestra with 1,000 violins playing in perfect harmony.

God's second great provision is His fulfillment of the certain truth of 1 Corinthians 10:13: "No temptation has overtaken you but such as is common to man; and God is faithful, who will not allow you to be tempted beyond what you are able, but with the temptation will provide the way of escape also, so that you will be able to endure it."

Every problem, trial, and painful experience you and I are asked to endure is "Father-filtered." You will not be tested beyond your ability to endure. In my darkest days, I thought my heart would break in two. It didn't! I only grew stronger, more empathetic, and more able to care for others in need.

A third great reassurance with which He equips you as you travel the "valley of the shadow of death" is that the trial is merely a shadow. It may look like death. Sometimes it may *feel* like death. But just as you'll find every time your car is passed on a highway by an 18-wheel semi truck, the shadow doesn't kill. A shadow is only a shadow.

As Franklin D. Roosevelt so aptly stated in his first inaugural address in 1933, "The only thing we have to fear is fear itself."

God's fourth mighty endowment bequeathed to His children living in "the dark night of the soul" is the gift of an "all-access backstage pass" into the heart of a friend who is experiencing the same affliction. This is my most blessed ability for which I'm the most thankful. As 2 Corinthians 1:4 promises, the value of understanding another's wounded heart far exceeds any pain I've been asked to endure. No one knows how to counsel or console a friend in crisis like a friend who has traveled the same road before.

If that's not enough, the summation of it all is, as my

daddy's favorite song proclaims, the greatest gift of all! Pain, through faith, always results in "just a closer walk with Thee."

What the Super Bowl championship is to the NFL player; what the 50-karat diamond is to the crown of a queen; what a 360-inch, seven-by-seven bull elk is to the archery hunter, the grand prize of suffering is to the closeness of Jesus. Face-to-face, eye-to-eye, heart-to-heart, father to son and father to daughter; this is the grandest gift of a lifetime.

Paul's words are again explicit and accurate: "Thanks be to God for His indescribable gift!" (2 Corinthians 9:15).

KNOWING GOD BY MAKING DISCIPLES

THE EMOTIONS IN THE ROOM were as thick and dark as a rain-saturated cloud on the front end of a November Kansas storm. Questions, fear, and insecurity filled the minds of 12 men who had left everything and invested their faith, their future, and their eternity in the One who identified Himself as "the Anointed One" of Daniel's historic and highly revered prophecy.

Just four days prior, Jesus had presented Himself as King as He rode into Jerusalem on a donkey, fulfilling Zechariah's prophecy about the Messiah (see Zechariah 9:9). The people, fulfilling David's prophecy in Psalm 118:26, had cried out, "Hosanna! Blessed is He who comes in the name of the Lord" (Mark 11:9).

Now the end had arrived. It was time for Jesus to bid His friends adieu. John recorded Jesus' words in great detail in chapters 13 to 17 of his gospel. In these five chapters, well worth the time and effort to memorize and meditate on, Jesus poured out His heart.

As you ponder these affectionately spoken words, you will become a dinner guest in that upper room as He describes God's plan for a crucifixion, a resurrection, an ascension, and a giving of the indwelling Holy Spirit. After Jesus washed the dusty feet of the men whom He had loved, walked with, and invested Himself in, He clearly communicated the difficulty of the road ahead while assuring them their ultimate victory had already been won.

"These things I have spoken to you, so that in Me you may have peace. In the world you have tribulation, but take courage; I have overcome the world" (John 16:33).

His words of promise, hope, and ultimate victory mean as much to His sincere followers of the twenty-first century as they did to those of the first.

Love is the theme of those five monumental chapters of Scripture, of John's carefully written account of those final hours of Jesus' life with His chosen 12. Hear Jesus' love as His small family of faith reclined at the table for their final meal together. Here's my paraphrase of Jesus' conversation on that historic night.

"In My love for you, My body will be broken for you in the same way I will break this bread before you."

"In My love for you, my blood will be poured out for you in the same way I pour this wine into the cup."

"In My love for you, I will send you My Spirit to make you brave and bring you peace."

"In My love for you, I'm going to go to the cross and endure great suffering."

"In My love for you, I will come back to life again as a testimony of your resurrection after your death."

"In My love for you, I'm going to ascend to My Father, where I will build for you a mansion, so we can live in the same neighborhood together *forever*."

And He proclaimed,

If you love Me, you will keep My commandments.
JOHN 14:15

He who has My commandments and keeps them is the one who loves Me.
JOHN 14:21

If anyone loves Me, he will keep My word.
JOHN 14:23

Love is complete when it's a two-way street. There are far too many parents in this world who give relentlessly to their children without building an environment of discipline, respect, and gratitude. This imbalance almost always creates a sense of entitlement, greed, and ingratitude. In the less politically correct world I grew up in, we called those kids "spoiled brats."

It's a tragedy that in twenty-first-century "Christianity," churches are filled with self-proclaimed Christians who are thrilled to lavish themselves in God's grace while neglecting God's call for worship and obedience.

Perhaps the greatest failing of those who claim to be Christ-followers is to use the oxymoron, "No, Lord." (I confess, I have uttered those two words many times in my 67 years of life.)

Jesus told His followers as He tells us today, "If anyone

does not abide in Me, he is thrown away as a branch and dries up; and they gather them, and cast them into the fire and they are burned" (John 15:6).

"If you call me Lord and practice lawlessness, I don't know you" (Matthew 7:23, paraphrased).

A long-term marriage is about as vivid a picture of Jesus' love as two people can get this side of heaven. The DNA of my 43-year-long marriage to the love of my life is that we bend over backward to try to please each other. I *love* making that girl smile!

We've gone through rain, hail, sleet, and snow together, and we still hold hands at night and even exchange an occasional kiss. Happy marriages are found by couples who each give 100 percent. My bride is so completely devoted to Jesus that He fills her with enough grace to humble herself about 20 notches and love me 100 percent. I am the "luckiest duck" on earth to be married far above what I deserve, so it's easy for me to love her 100 percent. One hundred percent love demands nothing in return. Fifty-fifty arrangements end up in separate bedrooms. As it is with marriage, so it is with knowing Jesus.

Considering *all* Jesus has done to say "I love you" to us, He asks for very little in return.

"Love your neighbor as you love yourself."

"Put God first in everything you do."

"Treat your body as a temple of the Holy Spirit."

"Pursue holiness."

"Talk to me about everything."

"Pray for the person who gossips about you."

"Feed the poor. Care for the less fortunate."

Scripture describes numerous ways to express our love to the One who exchanged His righteousness for our sin while trading in His lofty throne in heaven for six hours on a Roman cross.

LAST WORDS

I believe Jesus saved His favorite command for last. It's the one He lived out to its fullest. It's the one He modeled most consistently. This one was His lifestyle. He poured His life into it! They're the most-quoted, most-revered, and most-world-changing "famous last words" ever spoken: "Go therefore and make disciples" (Matthew 28:19).

Why did He save the best for last? Think about it.

If He spoke to you audibly and asked you to spend the rest of your life as an evangelist, and you would be speaking to 10,000 people every night, 365 days a year, and He told you that *all* 10,000 would trust Christ as their Savior, wouldn't that be a great adventure? Wouldn't that be a fantastic calling? Wouldn't you seize the opportunity and obey His command with enthusiasm?

As world-changing as that calling may sound, the results would actually be miniscule in terms of changing the world in your lifetime. You see, at that rate it would take you more than 2,000 years to reach the world with this all-important message.

On the other hand, if you were to engage *just one* person a year and "love him or her to Jesus" until that person is ready to love another to Jesus, and you were to continue that for another year and then another and another, while each person you had poured into did the same, do you know how long it would take to reach every person in the world?

Just 34 years.

It would take only 34 years to reach the world, not just with Christian converts, but with disciples. Perhaps that's why the word *Christian* is used in Scripture only three times, while the word *disciple* is used more than 250 times!

Jesus' command was to build reproducers who can build reproducers. Go invest in one, two, or a precious few at a time who will be biblically equipped to do the same for others.

There's a revealing fable of a wise man of antiquity who invented the game of chess. One day he shared his invention with a wealthy king. The king was so enthralled, he asked the inventor for a price so he could own the game in its entirety. The inventor shrewdly said, as he pointed to the lower left square on the board, "I'll take one grain of wheat for this square."

Then, before the king had time to respond, the inventor pointed to the next square and said, "The price for this square is double the grains of wheat on the previous square." The inventor then moved his finger carefully to the third, fourth, fifth, and sixth squares and asked the king to simply double the grains of wheat demanded on the previous square.

Finally, he placed his finger on the upper right square, the sixty-fourth and last square, and exclaimed, "The price for this entire game is the number of grains of wheat accumulated on *all these* squares."

The king enthusiastically and naively cried out, "I'll do it! It's a deal!" The king did not know how to rule mathematics as well as he knew how to rule people. The number of grains required to pay for just the last square was two to the sixty-third power, which is more than nine quintillion. For the entire chessboard, the price would be two to the 2,016th power, plus one! That's more than 43 quintillion—43 followed by 18 zeroes!

"GO THEREFORE AND MAKE DISCIPLES . . ."

Of all the 84 Promise Keepers events at which I was asked to speak, my favorite, by far, was the smallest event of all. The crowd would number only 1,400 men. Most of them would be murderers, rapists, serial killers, and armed robbers locked away behind carefully supervised concrete walls with steel-barred windows and surrounded by tall, electrified, barbed-wire fences.

Before I went, I heard the inmates had been praying for three years that we would come to their high-security prison to do the four-hour event.

I could not wait to fulfill the invitation.

Walking into the prison with my double-bladed 4-foot ax, 2½-pound sledgehammer, and 5⅜" x 12" steel spikes required for the building-the-cross drama I would perform was awkward, to say the least!

Going through checkpoint after checkpoint, one electrically locked door after another, I noticed a surprisingly warm and friendly attitude from everyone I met. When we arrived in the prison yard, I was amazed to see the grass and flowers meticulously manicured, the prison in perfect peace, and the guards and inmates harmonizing like an orchestra.

When the warden, Ms. Chris Money, was introduced, the 1,400 inmates who were gathered in front of the speaking platform gave her a standing ovation. The first order of business was the arrival of Ms. Money's 80-man "silent choir." Tears flowed profusely from my eyes as these men, once hardened criminals, signed with their hands as if communicating to the hearing-impaired, to multiple Christian worship songs. Their faces glowed like those of angels.

"Irish Johnny" followed the silent choir with a stirring,

10-minute testimony of his past life as a murderer and leader of the Aryan Society, the most notorious racist group in this prison. As "Irish Johnny" returned to his seat, the African-American inmates gave him a standing ovation. To say I was deeply moved would be the greatest understatement of my life.

I performed the drama of the Roman soldier and the cross. At the invitation, some 1,200 inmates stood to express their solidarity in surrender to the lordship of Christ.

For four wonderful hours, we fellowshipped and worshiped together in the prison yard. I gave long, emotional, fatherly hugs and a father's blessing to as many of the men as I could get my hands on.

As I lingered in amazement at the peace that permeated the prison crowd, the backstory emerged about why this transformation occurred in a prison once known for its rioting.

Apparently, six years before the event, six laymen from a local church started visiting the prison regularly. Each Christian man took one inmate and, as they described it, "loved a man to Jesus until he was ready to love a man to Jesus." Then, with the blessing of the warden, they would change cells, and now 12 men would duplicate what the six men had begun. In a matter of months, there were 24, then 48, and then 96. As the years passed, this "first-century discipleship" pattern had transformed an entire prison into a Christ-centered family.

Paul's words to Timothy in 2 Timothy 2:2 had come to full fruition: "The things which you have heard from me in the presence of many witnesses, entrust these to faithful men who will be able to teach others also."

God spoke heavily to my spirit as I exited those prison walls and recalled those never-to-be-forgotten hours. It was as if God were saying, "If this can happen inside a prison, why can't it happen in America? Why not the world?" Jesus knew the world-changing power of disciple making as He poured His life into 12 men. Paul did the same with Timothy and Epaphroditus. Peter obediently followed suit with Sylvanus.

As I travel to churches to do events across America and around the world, I tragically see little of what I saw in Marion prison. I see large, elaborate, meaningful Sunday morning services, well-planned Sunday school classes, and even house groups and Bible studies. But the intentional pattern of "reproducing reproducers" through deliberate discipleship is largely a lost art.

In May 2015, the Barna Research Group released a disappointing telltale study. In partnership with Navpress, they had completed a remarkably comprehensive survey on "The State of Discipleship."[1] Through careful studies with 933 multi-denominational pastors, it was first revealed that only 1 percent believed today's churches are doing well at discipling new and young believers. Additionally, the survey said 60 percent of the pastors reported that *their* church was "not doing very well" in this endeavor.

The survey was also extended to church-goers across the nation. After qualifying another 2,013 individual surveys, a whopping 77 percent believed that it's "very important to see growth in their spiritual life," but only 17 percent met with a spiritual mentor and experienced the growth potential found in Paul-Timothy discipleship.

Sadly, even in the tiny fraction of churches that do discipleship on any significant level, of the 13 components of disciple-making benefits offered in the survey, "the study of the Bible" came in eleventh place.

In Dallas Willard's insightful book *The Great Omission*, he stated, "The New Testament is a book about disciples, by disciples, for disciples of Jesus Christ."[2] Willard defined a disciple as "a learner, a student, an apprentice—a practitioner even if only a beginner." Disciples of Jesus are people who do not just profess certain views but also *apply* their growing understanding of life in the Kingdom of heaven to every aspect of life on earth. "The disciple is one who, intending to become Christ-like and so dwelling in his 'faith and practice,' systematically and progressively rearranges his affairs to that end."[3]

Willard went on to say, "It is a tragic error to think that Jesus was telling us, as he left, to start churches, as that is understood today. *He told us as disciples to make disciples, not converts to Christianity*" (emphasis added).[4]

Willard then concluded his beautiful treatise with this summary: "Our directions 'as we go' are clear. Be disciples—apprentices of Jesus in kingdom living and by our life and words as his apprentices to witness, to bring others to know and long for the life that is in us through confidence in Him. It's all true. It works. It is accessible to anyone and there's nothing in the world to compare."[5]

Acts 8:4 describes the explosion of the first-century church with these words: "Therefore, those who had been scattered went about preaching the word." In John S. Dickerson's extraordinary work *The Great Evangelical Recession*, he stated, "Our evangelical engine is not sputtering for lack of big events, but because it's low on individual believers actually explaining the gospel, from the platform of a life that earns the right to speak."[6]

"He who is wise wins souls" (Proverbs 11:30).

Shortly before I met him, Jake was standing on top of a water tower with a fifth of whiskey in his hand, mustering the courage to leap to his sudden death. Although he had made that climb three times, intending to end his life each time, he fortunately never took the leap. Even though he suffered from depression and self-defeat, he was able to carry out his golf course job duties.

I first met Jake one fall afternoon while he helped me load my clubs onto a cart. Within five minutes, the Lord opened the door to a deep, spiritual place where Jake had never before traveled. I carefully explained God's grace and the pathway to salvation in Jesus Christ. As Jake and I prayed together, a certain peace fell on that dear young man.

We began to meet weekly and study the *LifeLine* discipleship book together. Jake became a young professional, a faithful husband, and caring father. The day I saw Jake, his wife, and their two-year-old daughter in church on a Sunday morning, four years after we first met, was a truly touching moment.

Over the years, the joy of my life—God's intention for the joy of *every* believer's life—continues to be to make disciples of all the Jakes who cross my path.

Although I can't come close to his wisdom, courage, or dedication, I relate to the apostle Paul in so many ways. I feel as he did, like the most undeserving of all to be captured by God's grace. I, like him, feel as though I'm "the chief of sinners" and least worthy of all believers. Through countless failures, God has assured me that apart from Christ I can accomplish nothing of value. Disciple making does not require perfect men and women. Loving someone to Jesus only requires sincere, Christ-following men and women who are willing.

But, like Paul, I'm passionate about seeking, finding, and

discipling young Timothys and "loving a man to Jesus until he's ready to love a man to Jesus." This is the greatest privilege of life. I *always* get so much more out of my time with my Timothys than they do. And the highest treasure both of us receive is a greater, more tender, and more intimate love for the One whose life we seek to follow.

Disciple making is the greenhouse of intimacy. It's here, in developing Christ-followers through intentional Bible-based relationships, sharing His irresistible love that won us over, that a believer begins to experience the tender, affectionate, fulfilling walk with Jesus that He intends for every disciple.

Paul, in writing to the Thessalonian church he so dearly loved, described his God-ordained vision of his moment of transformation into the presence of Jesus and the presentation of his "victor's crown": "For who is our hope or joy or crown of exultation? Is it not even you, in the presence of our Lord Jesus at His coming? For you are our glory and joy" (1 Thessalonians 2:19-20).

Through divine revelation, Paul saw that his greatest eternal reward in the moment he met Christ face-to-face would be having Timothy stand with him as Jesus received him into His eternal presence. Can anything in our quest for fulfillment be better than that?

For your own, free, lifetime usage and enjoyment as you strive to make disciples, I have compiled the wisdom of my spiritual mentors into a book that can easily appear on your and your Timothys' smartphones, iPads, and computers. It's all in a free app. This "add water and stir" discipleship plan requires no previous homework. The only requirement is that you and your Timothy show up with lives ready to be transformed by the Word of God. When you begin to pray for your Timothys, you'll find them lining up like airplanes on a runway in the airport of your mind.

All credit for the studies goes to my mentors Dr. Howard Hendricks, Kay Arthur, Dr. Bill Bright, Max Lucado, Dr. Gary Smalley, Josh McDowell, Ken Poure, Dr. Adrian Rogers, Jack Herschend, and my dad.

The app versions are Apple and Android friendly. The studies are specifically designed for woman-to-woman, man-to-man, student-to-student, or parent-to-child relationships. Just go to your app store, locate "LifeLine 9Eleven," and follow the pathway described. Grab your favorite cup of coffee, invite a Timothy, and prepare yourself for the greatest adventure of your life!

For you and your children, or for you and your Timothy, I've also provided a daily video devotional app called "FUEL UP," currently available for download. This app can even serve as an alarm clock that will pop up on your smartphone each day at a time you (and your Timothy) have set. The streaming charges on this app are only 99 cents per month.

The "joy of the Lord," the "depth of the Lord," and "the victor's crown" await your enthusiastic participation.

"Shepherd the flock of God among you, exercising oversight not under compulsion, but voluntarily, according to the will of God; and not for sordid gain, but with eagerness; nor yet as lording it over those allotted to your charge, but proving to be examples to the flock. And when the Chief Shepherd appears, you will receive the unfading crown of glory" (1 Peter 5:2-4).

11

HELP FROM
THE HOLY SPIRIT

I REMEMBER LIKE IT WAS YESTERDAY, enduring the horrific pregame jitters in Memorial Stadium in Austin, Texas, as our head coach, Hayden Fry, gave his last motivational speech before we faced the national champion Texas Longhorns. I doubt Coach Fry knew how afraid I felt when he told us they had won 37 games in a row and were, undoubtedly, the best college football team in the country. I played nose man on defense, and my assignment put me at the tip of the spear of the Longhorns' high-octane triple option offense.

I recalled that moment as the pre-op nurse left my hospital room after giving me the "pregame" speech for the next day's open-heart surgery. I felt as if I were back in Austin. Back then, the jitters were about a 60-minute football game. On that day in the hospital, it was about life and death.

A lot has happened in my life since Darrell Royal and his

burnt orange stampede took the field and repeatedly ran over my helpless body in those days of Longhorn glory.

Yes, the stakes of the operation were higher than those of a football game, but the vitality of my relationship with Jesus was also stronger than in the old days. He is a great partner during life's many practice sessions, but when it's "game time," He's at His best.

I knew before the procedure that as I kissed my wife good-bye and went under for a four-hour "adventure" into the depths of the one muscle my body can't live without, I *would* have peace.

It's a win-win deal.

Yes, the odds were I would wake up and continue to live in God's countless blessings with a big, lost world to reach with the cross. But the day before, as I "buckled up my chin strap" and prepared to "take the field" for the biggest game of my life, I could relate to the apostle Paul's words written to the Philippian church. With shackles on his hands and feet, he wrote, "For to me, to live is Christ and to die is gain" (Philippians 1:21).

I knew that the Holy Spirit would deliver courage in the operating room. He is the One Jesus promised to you the night you first believed. Through faith, you joined the 11 faithful followers in that famed upper room the night before Jesus' crucifixion as He promised, "I will not leave you as orphans; I will come to you" (John 14:18). He also offered words of promise on that infamous Thursday night, saying, "I will ask the Father, and He will give you another Helper, that He may be with you forever" (John 14:16).

"He will guide you into all the truth" (John 16:13).

"He will be your Helper" (John 14:26, paraphrased).

"He will disclose to you what is to come" (John 16:13).

"He . . . will convict the world concerning sin and righteousness and judgment" (John 16:8).

"He will testify about Me [Jesus]" (John 15:26).

"He will glorify Me" (John 16:14).

"He will produce fruit in your life" (Galatians 5:22, paraphrased).

"He will give gifts to you" (1 Corinthians 12:7, paraphrased).

"He will empower you to be His witness" (Acts 1:8, paraphrased).

In other words, the Holy Spirit is the One who makes possible our journey to the heart of Jesus on a daily basis.

According to the Barclay Bible commentary, as "the Comforter," the Holy Spirit (Greek *Parakletos*) speaks a word of bravery to a defeated army to give His warriors the courage to go back into the battle again. I was *positive* that in 24 hours I would have those words of bravery, as the Holy Spirit has been *so* faithful to speak them in previous times of tragedy and trial.

BORROWED COURAGE

The Kansas City Chiefs football team was founded by Lamar Hunt in 1960 as the cornerstone of the new American Football League, which eventually merged with the NFL. Upon the founder's death in 2006, Clark Hunt, Lamar's son, became the CEO.

Although the Chiefs have won only one Super Bowl in their 50-plus-year existence, the 76,416 seats of Arrowhead Stadium are almost always filled with loyal fans who reportedly create more game-day noise than any other crowd in the league.

The third floor of the Marriott hotel in downtown Kansas City is always buzzing with players and coaches the Saturday night before a Sunday afternoon home game, as the Chiefs make final preparations for the upcoming contest.

In the midst of the pregame meetings and lavish smorgasbord dining, a 30-minute time slot is reserved for a chapel service. In the disappointing early season of 2015, I was invited to speak at the Chiefs' chapel the night before the Chicago Bears game. The Chiefs had won only one game at that point, while losing three.

Sitting quietly in the service that evening was an unmistakably bald player named Eric Berry. An All-Pro defensive safety, Eric was recovering from an extremely taxing year of chemotherapy treatments that had arrested his non-Hodgkin lymphoma (cancer).

The Chiefs-Bears game the next day was a disaster. The Chiefs played poorly on both sides of the ball. With nine minutes left in the third quarter, I was standing by Clark Hunt's side with my hand on his shoulder in fatherly affection. When his All-Pro running back, Jamaal Charles, went down with a badly torn ACL, I felt Clark's heart tremble. What little hope the Chiefs' fans brought to the stadium that day died as the team doctors and trainers assisted their superstar to the sideline.

To the astonishment of fans, players, and coaches across the nation, the unthinkable transpired over the following weeks. The Chiefs accomplished what no team had ever done before. In spite of a five-loss beginning, the team won 10 straight games and made it into the playoffs.

I asked Clark and team chaplain Phillip Kelly to tell me the "why" behind this mystery. How did the Chiefs pull off the seemingly impossible comeback?

Both Clark and Phillip pointed to the same answer—Eric Berry. Though quiet by nature, Eric spoke up in the weeks after the loss to the Bears with a voice of unparalleled respect in the locker room: "The reason I came back this season was to be with the team, my family, to show you that if I can come back from cancer, you can come back from *anything*."

Eric's faith in God and in his team began the greatest comeback in NFL history. His "word of bravery," the comfort of the Holy Spirit that God's Word promises to those who endure hardship so they can give the same word to others going through hardship, redirected the future for an entire football franchise.

How much more can He do the same through you! Chiefs chaplain Phillip Kelly calls it "borrowed courage."

When my children were under our roof, we memorized a lot of Scripture. At age three, during "lay by time" before bed, they began to memorize verses, and by age seven they were memorizing chapters. By age 10, they had started to memorize books.

Watching your kids turn 16 can be horrific for a parent who is savvy to the perilous influence of the twenty-first-century teenage world. When they start to go on dates and to parties, you can't always join them. But fortunately, the Holy Spirit guides them into truth when they know the Bible. Jesus promised He will "bring to your remembrance all that I said to you" (John 14:26).

On a Focus on the Family radio broadcast, my teenage daughter, Courtney, hit the nail on the head when she was asked, "Do you remember every verse you have memorized with your dad?"

She said something along these lines: "No, not every word, but when I need them God brings them to my mind." I asked her the same question one night during her early adolescence. She responded forthrightly, "When a girl is in junior high, she has a lot of difficult decisions to make. When she has God's Word in her heart, she doesn't have to go home and look it up."

If you're fighting with self-doubt, anger, lust, depression, defeat, fear of abandonment, guilt, or shame in this season of your life, perhaps you'll want to enlist the Holy Spirit as your Counselor and let Him speak to you with great reassurance.

Through countless, cherished years of counseling hurting hearts, I have learned there are two radio stations playing in your mind. Both of them are "on the air" 24 hours a day, seven days a week, 365 days a year. One station is called "The Lie." You can be absolutely positive that everything aired on that broadcast is meant to defeat you and rob you of your joy. The "DJ" of station "The Lie," as you might guess, is Satan himself. His IQ is about 7,000. He knows your weaknesses better than you do. He loves to take you down and then keep you there as long as you tune him in.

"You can't . . ."

"You'll never escape this one."

"You deserve to be angry."

"You'll never get over it, so why try?"

"God betrayed you, so why trust Him now?"

"If you're 'in love,' it's okay to . . ."

"You are such a disappointment."

"You failed before, you'll fail again."

"There's no use trying."

"God is *really* upset with you."

"You're not worthy of God's love."

Sound familiar?

Fortunately, there's another radio station that can play in your mind with far more life-changing volume. This other station is called "The Great I AM." It, too, plays 24 hours a day, seven days a week, 365 days a year. The "DJ" is the Holy Spirit. He speaks to His adopted sons and daughters through His Word. He always tells the truth. He always lifts you up. He points out deceit and the pitfalls of harmful temptations while assuring the believer of God's unrelenting grace and limitless power. His mercies are "new every morning" (Lamentations 3:23).

When God made man and woman in His own image (see Genesis 1:27), He put your hands on the radio dial. You get to tune in to either radio station you choose.

When the Holy Spirit recalls Scripture to your mind, you can adjust your attitude and actions, or you can "quench the Spirit" or "grieve the Spirit" by changing the station back to "The Lie." To quench the Spirit, you refuse His voice and "put out the fire" of truth and life that speaks to you. To grieve the Spirit is to actually hurt Him by rejecting His counsel as He instructs you in order to protect and provide for your well-being.

"Do not grieve the Holy Spirit of God, by whom you were sealed for the day of redemption" (Ephesians 4:30).

"Do not quench the Spirit" (1 Thessalonians 5:19).

The late Dr. Bill Bright was the single greatest visionary I ever met. He was fond of our sports camps, and I was fond of him. His Campus Crusade for Christ worldwide movement of evangelism and discipleship has reached literally hundreds of millions in every conceivable sociological environment on earth, from the most remote tribal villages in South America or Africa to the largest metroplexes in the Western world.

Dr. Bright was also a great writer. One of his bedrock teaching series was known as his "transferable concepts." I ate them up like a good peanut butter and jelly sandwich. One of his booklets, titled "Walking in the Spirit," is truly a masterpiece. This method of practical daily living is a minute-by-minute plan to bring Paul's exhortation in Galatians down on the bottom shelf where it's readily accessible.

"But I say, walk by the Spirit, and you will not carry out the desire of the flesh" (Galatians 5:16).

Romans 8:5-11 lays out a convincing argument for the importance of a believer's daily walk:

> For those who are according to the flesh set their minds on the things of the flesh, but those who are according to the Spirit, the things of the Spirit. For the mind set on the flesh is death, but the mind set on the Spirit is life and peace, because the mind set on the flesh is hostile toward God; for it does not subject itself to the law of God, for it is not even able to do so, and those who are in the flesh cannot please God.
>
> However you are not in the flesh but in the Spirit, if indeed the Spirit of God dwells in you. But if anyone does not have the Spirit of Christ, he does not belong to Him. If Christ is in you, though the body is dead because of sin, yet the spirit is alive because of righteousness. But if the Spirit of Him who raised Jesus from the dead dwells in you, He who raised Christ Jesus from the dead will also give life to your mortal bodies through His Spirit who dwells in you.

As that passage says, the day you give your life to Jesus, not simply by a prayer or showing up to church on Sunday but by surrendering your life to follow Him and put Him first, you are immediately given the gift of the Holy Spirit. Romans 10:9-10 echoes this truth and provides great reassurance for every sincere Christ-follower: "that if you confess with your mouth Jesus as Lord, and believe in your heart that God raised Him from the dead, you will be saved; for with the heart a person believes, resulting in righteousness, and with the mouth he confesses, resulting in salvation."

Dr. Bright taught that even though the believer has the Holy Spirit living inside him or her, the Christ-follower can be "filled" with the Spirit of Christ by a prayer of dedicated faith: "Lord, fill me with Your Spirit."

Robert Munger, in his best-selling book *My Heart— Christ's Home*, pictured this prayer of sincere dedication as the day a believer gives "the keys and deed" of his "home-shaped" heart to Jesus. At that moment, Munger wrote, you not only give Jesus the inside of your heart one room at a time, but you also ask Him to be Lord and Master of everything you were, are, and forever will be.[1]

The apostle Paul taught it this way: "And do not get drunk with wine, for that is dissipation, but be filled with the Spirit" (Ephesians 5:18). The verb translated *filled*, in the original Greek of the New Testament, is in the present perfect tense. So the verse actually says, "Be continually being filled" with the Spirit of Christ.

To be "filled" is far more than an emotional or religious experience. It means to be empowered by the Holy Spirit, to walk under His authority, to think under His authority, to love and treat others under His authority, and to make daily decisions under His authority.

The Spirit-filled life, simply put, is a life lived joyfully and submissively under the lordship of Christ.

THE THRILL OF FREEDOM

It's thrilling to watch the freedom new believers experience when they no longer have a yoke of sin. I get to watch this "birthing" process each time I do the cross-builder presentation on a college campus. Drug addictions, abortions, rapes, alcohol and porn addictions, and bitterness flood the cross each night like the mighty Mississippi River as students repent and give their lives to follow Jesus.

"It was for freedom that Christ set us free" (Galatians 5:1).

Dr. Bright presented a revolutionary idea when he referred to the Spirit-filled daily walk as "spiritual breathing." Satan is such a *constant* voice of temptation and failure. But because Jesus defeated him 2,000 years ago on a Roman cross, His Spirit can rule when a believer exhales confession and inhales the fullness of that Spirit.

We recognize our sinful thoughts and exhale, "Lord, forgive me. That's wrong, and I'm sorry." Then we inhale, "Holy Spirit, fill me."

When we do that, the great exhortation of 2 Corinthians 10:5 is ours to experience. "We are taking every thought captive to the obedience of Christ." The Spirit-filled life through spiritual breathing conquers bitterness, porn addiction, outbursts of anger, the use of explosive language, self-deprivation, and self-degradation under the guiding hand of Jesus Christ.

The bondage is broken, and it *stays* broken. The sin is forgiven, and it *stays* forgiven.

Yes, spiritual breathing is a discipline that a believer who wants to walk in freedom and fellowship with Jesus must submit to with every cell in his or her body. Yes, it takes an all-out commitment to the Spirit's filling. Yes, it takes relentless practice to make it a way of life. But if God is for you, who can stop you? If Jesus stands in the gap for you, who can defeat you? If the Holy Spirit reigns in your life, who can overcome you?

The promises of Romans 8, "the chapter of golden virtues," are yours to behold. Embrace them, memorize them, claim them, and live in them:

"He who did not spare His own Son, but delivered Him over for us all, how will He not also with Him freely give us all things?" (Romans 8:32).

"For I am convinced that neither death, nor life, nor angels, nor principalities, nor things present, nor things to come, nor powers, nor height, nor depth, nor any other created thing, will be able to separate us from the love of God, which is in Christ Jesus our Lord" (Romans 8:38-39).

WALKING IN THE SPIRIT

My son Brady pastors a church for Disney cast members at Walt Disney World in Orlando, Florida. Some say his wife, Jennafer, looks a lot like Cinderella, but at times she looks like Aurora, Belle, or Mary Poppins. All I know is that not only do little girls flock to get a picture with her every day, but also fellow cast members, with whom she leads Bible studies between parades and shows, think she looks a lot like Jesus. Her kind and unselfish way of living makes her look a lot like Jesus to me, too.

Brady loves to brag on his Jennafer. He treats her like a true Cinderella and loves her for sharing Jesus. "She sees the best in everyone," he says. "Jennafer sees every person she meets through lenses of love."

Brady teaches me a whole lot more than I teach him. His wisdom and contagious sense of humor overflow each Sunday night as he leads his church filled with big, puppy-eyed Disney princess lookalikes, Mickeys, Minnies, Goofys, Plutos, Peter Pans, food service employees, ride operators, custodians, and other assorted Disney characters who have learned to walk with Jesus through his and Jennafer's example.

Recently, Brady taught me a great viewpoint on how to walk in the Spirit every day for the rest of my life. He calls it "looking at life through lenses of love." Just as a fine pair of polarized Ray-Ban or Maui Jim sunglasses filters out reflections that inhibit a clean view of a sunset sparkling in the ocean, so also lenses of love filter out the blinding reflections of life caused by pride.

You and I get to choose which sunglasses we want to put on each day.

Lenses of love see the people in our lives with patience, kindness, a lack of jealousy, a lack of bragging, a lack of arrogance, and a lack of seeking our own way. They cause us to speak and act like the people of purity we are in Jesus and to live with dedication to following His truths.

The other lenses that can be placed in your sunglass frames are lenses of pride. Lenses of pride see girls and women as sex objects to be conquered and less-fortunate people or people of diverse race as lower class.

Lenses of pride ask, "What's in it for me?" Lenses of love ask, "How can I serve you to make your life better?" Lenses of love are secured by getting to know God through His Word. Lenses of pride are put in place by the adversary.

The astounding wonder, the diamond on the king's crown, the greatest of all the virtues of Scripture is to walk in the Spirit from the center of one's heart to the thoughts one thinks, the words one says, and the actions one takes. This type of life produces the fruit of the Spirit as Galatians 5:22-23 becomes who you are: "The fruit of the Spirit is love, joy, peace, patience, kindness, goodness, faithfulness, gentleness, self-control; against such things there is no law."

That's our Jennafer. That's the heart of Mosaic Church in Walt Disney World, which has helped change the attitudes of people in the princess gowns and character costumes from one of selfishness, jealousy, and greed to one of loving, serving, and seeing each other through lenses of love.

That can become the story of your home. That's why Paul used the term *indescribable* for the gift of the Holy Spirit: "Thanks be to God for His indescribable gift!" (2 Corinthians 9:15).

FACING FORWARD

Many years ago, I read a simple, four-panel "Peanuts" comic strip in which Lucy spoke candidly to Charlie Brown. As they stood on the front of a giant ocean liner, Lucy said in her matter-of-fact way, "Charlie, some people sit on the front of the ship and see where the ship is going."

In the second panel, Lucy and Charlie were sitting on the side of the ship and Lucy proclaimed, "Charlie, some people sit on the side of the ship and see things as they pass by."

Moving to the third panel, we saw Lucy and Charlie sitting on the back of the ship. Lucy continued, "Charlie, some people sit at the back of the ship and watch where they've been."

The fourth panel was brief and ever so insightful. Lucy looked at Charlie and simply asked, "Which way is your chair facing today, Charlie Brown?"

The Holy Spirit takes you to the "front of the ship," where you can navigate life with hope and peace. He guides you into truth like an underground cave guide with a vibrant halogen light piercing the darkness ahead. He speaks through

Paul in Philippians 3:13-14 to tell you in your most challenging journey, "But one thing I do: forgetting what lies behind and reaching forward to what lies ahead, I press on toward the goal for the prize of the upward call of God in Christ Jesus."

There were only 10 minutes left before they wheeled me off to the most difficult surgery of my life, yet I experienced the Holy Spirit's comfort and peace. The Great I Am said He would guide the surgeon's hands and heal my wounded heart.

The pre-op interlude was "game time," when faith became experience, the theoretical became practical, and the Spirit of God became my every breath. I had left the locker room and stepped into the arena.

12

KNOWING GOD THROUGH FAITH

THE 28 DAYS following my open heart surgery and subsequent lung surgery, with the excruciating pain, unrelenting nausea, and long, sleepless nights, were part of the medical package that made Psalm 139 come alive in a way I'd never experienced before. The words of Psalm 139:11-12 were very real to me: "If I say, 'Surely the darkness will overwhelm me, and the light around me will be night,' even the darkness is not dark to You, and the night is as bright as the day. Darkness and light are alike to You."

The reliable truth of David's words in Psalm 62:5-7 guided me through the day: "My soul, wait in silence for God only, for my hope is from Him. He only is my rock and my salvation, my stronghold; I shall not be shaken. On God my salvation and my glory rest; the rock of my strength, my refuge is in God."

Likewise, Psalm 63:6-8 sustained my soul through the never-ending nighttime hours: "When I remember You on my bed, I meditate on You in the night watches, for You have been my help, and in the shadow of Your wings I sing for joy. My soul clings to You; Your right hand upholds me."

Going home to my superstar wife and my faithful, golden-eyed chocolate labrador retriever, Koda, was indescribably exhilarating. After 28 days, my legs could walk again—though my short, deliberate steps were topsy-turvy. My eyes could see the springtime Ozark wildflower display covering the hills like a Fourth of July fireworks celebration. The bluebird, robin, belted kingfisher, and great blue heron celebrated the iridescent blue sky and Ozark sunshine in the warm breeze. To me, each uniquely colorful species looked like a Michelangelo masterpiece. I took my first few steps in the springtime grass bursting with purple sweet violets, golden dandelions, and bluebell-like speedwells that I had scarcely noticed before. Never had the colors seemed so splendid. Never had the elements of God's creation shouted out His artistic wonder with such symphonic orchestration. Never had Dorothy's words resounded so triumphantly in my ears, "There's no place like home!"

I reflected on the past redefining month of my life and could see with 20/20 vision God's hand of love and blessing in the brokenness and pain, and His healing power through every step of the journey.

JOLIE'S STORY

Late-night conversations with dedicated staff were the highlights of the entire experience. My most cherished friendship formed between 2:00 a.m. and 4:00 a.m. the last night of my hospitalization. I had never heard a personal story so intriguing as that of this 60-year-old nurse's aide who candidly told her life's tale by my bedside. "Nurse Jolie" was truly one of a kind in all the world. Her voice was gentle and reassuring as she gazed above me from her one functional eye; the other was missing because her mom contracted rubella during pregnancy. Her "dad" was a military man who wandered into the mom's bedroom as she coordinated a brothel in a small apartment just above a bar in San Francisco's "Tenderloin" district. Unable to cope with her own addictions and frailties, her mom was also incapable of raising her small, adventuresome toddler, offering only a few scraps of food during sporadic mealtimes.

Jolie's earliest memories were of playing unsupervised on the perilous sidewalks and in the streets and parking garages where drugs and prostitution were the stuff of everyday life.

Her faith journey, however, began at birth when the delivering physician told her mom this child was going to do something significant with her life. Beginning at age six, Jolie recalled being mysteriously drawn to neighborhood churches. Within a year, her independent footsteps landed in a small Lutheran church, where the Bible was explained in a way she could grasp with her immature mind. With nothing else to guide her except the very Spirit of God who constantly led her to walk with Jesus, Jolie pursued faith with zeal.

Jolie still remembers, throughout her childhood, seeking God in the Bible and finding a rich relationship with Jesus that filled the many gaps of fatherlessness and orphanlike survival.

"I sought the LORD, and He answered me, and delivered me from all my fears" (Psalm 34:4).

Jolie's reception of God's promise to guide seekers led her not only through her childhood, adolescence, and college, but even into graduate school, where she eventually earned a master's degree in divinity and became a sign language interpreter for the hearing impaired. Today, she faithfully serves as "undercover chaplain" in the hospital where she spreads Jesus' irresistible love and encourages and comforts lonely, hurting patients throughout the long and sometimes desperate nights.

THE ESSENCE OF FAITH

"Now faith is the assurance of things hoped for, the conviction of things not seen" (Hebrews 11:1).

The account of Jesus' dramatic interaction with the thief on the cross has always been one of the most intriguing and reassuring passages in all of Scripture. Here, amid the excruciating pain of crucifixion, Jesus, in His passion to seek and save the lost, found one more son to adopt before He sent His spirit upward and breathed His last breath.

Talk about drama—astounding, extraordinary drama! There on the stage of what is now the most revered hilltop in the world, Golgotha, hung three men. In the middle was the God-Man, Jesus, the hope and Savior of the world. Hanging beside Him on three blacksmith spikes, one in each wrist and one through the ankles, hung the two thieves. We don't know all their crimes against the gruesome authority of the Roman government, but we do know one thief was a scoffer, the other a seeker. The seeker took his tiny seed of faith and placed it in the heart of the only Man who could save him. The seed landed in the fertile soil of Jesus' relentless desire to adopt all those who, no matter how dire their circumstances, place their faith in Him for life and salvation.

The awful silence surrounding the last few gasping breaths of the six-hour torturous death was broken when the thief cried out, "Jesus, remember me when You come in Your kingdom!" (Luke 23:42).

Finding the only requirement for adoption, salvation, and eternal life satisfied, Jesus responded triumphantly, "Today you shall be with Me in Paradise" (23:43). You can almost hear Jesus' thoughts as He performed the last-minute adoption: *Yes, I'll remember you. Your faith has found a home in My heart. You're My son now. After this ordeal is over, I will introduce you to My Dad. You're going home with Me.*

Faith alone—no church service, no pomp, no ceremony, no religious activity, nothing to add. Faith alone in Christ alone—salvation.

Faith is simply believing without seeing, having confidence that God is sovereign, good, and faithful to His promises. Faith is relinquishing control to Him, resting fully assured that in the long run God's will for your life is best.

During the darkest, most painful and desperate night of my heart and lung surgeries, when I felt as if I were being tortured by water-boarding for hours, gasping for breath, an old acronym I learned as a youngster returned: FAITH (Father, All In Thy Hands). My "feelings" were numb. I felt zero connection to Him or anyone else. But in the anguish, I kept thinking, *Father, All In Thy Hands*, and it carried me through—always has, always will.

KELLEY'S STORY

My dear friend Kelley Brown is a woman of extraordinary faith. After losing her husband, Adam, a US Navy SEAL, in a heroic firefight in Afghanistan, Kelley dug into her bedrock foundation and clung to her faith in Jesus with all the strength she could muster. And she embraced the extended friendship of Adam's SEAL team, who stepped in to help.

Then the unthinkable happened. In another anti-terrorist mission, the helicopter carrying the SEAL team was struck by a rocket, and everyone on the team lost his life. Funeral after funeral awaited Kelley until she had attended 50 burials, including one for her mom.

Kelley, as a single mom, raises her teenagers and manages her household with Jesus as her husband and God as "the Father to the fatherless." She says, through humble eyes and a broken heart, "I'm so thankful my faith was intact when Adam died. I knew where to turn, so I ran to Jesus. I trusted Him to take care of my children." Kelley nurtures her faith each day as she steps into her own "war room" where she can, in her closet, spend undistracted time with Jesus. "There, in my 'war room,'" she says with a smile, "Jesus restores me every day."

She describes that stability through the seemingly unceasing series of personal loss: My faith is my foundation. People ask me why. I tell them I know God has a plan. His timing is perfect. He is never early, and He is never late. As difficult as life is, I believe my life is divinely orchestrated. Now I see that same faith in my kids. They are not afraid to live out their faith through their adolescent years. I know, without a doubt, that God will get us through."

THE TAPROOT OF BELIEF

Faith is the taproot of belief. Belief is the root system of salvation. Above the ground, you and those who truly know you see a tree of life that is changed; a life that puts Jesus first in everything; a life that intrinsically produces the fruit of the Spirit—love, joy, peace, patience, kindness, goodness, gentleness, faithfulness, and self-control.

I hired the defensive coordinator of my college football

team to come to Missouri and help me run the camp just after I graduated. I was young and inexperienced. I knew he could bring some much-needed wisdom and discipline to our staff. Coach Utley was the toughest coach I'd ever met, but he was loved by our team for his contagious personality and his caring heart for his players.

During staff training week that summer, Coach Utley and his seven-year-old son, Lee, were in our small ski boat, pulling a big guy on a slalom ski. When the skier cut hard from one side of the boat to the other, something happened that I've never seen before or since that fateful day. The boat flipped upside down, throwing Coach, Lee, and the driver overboard.

When Coach surfaced, he realized Lee wasn't with him, so he began to swim frantically around the boat, crying out Lee's name. There was no answer. Lee had apparently disappeared into the deep water below. In one last-ditch effort to find his son, Coach ducked under the capsized boat and popped up in the air pocket created by the sides of the boat as it lay "turtled" on top of the water. Miraculously, Lee was treading water in that air pocket, waiting for his daddy to find him.

The reunion was exhilarating, to say the least. Hugs, tears, and words of joy and affection were exchanged. Coach then swam Lee to the shore in grateful silence. As the reunited father and son walked up the hill to their cabin, Coach cradled Lee in his arms.

After a few minutes, Coach asked Lee, "Son, were you scared?"

Lee returned a warm smile and said, "I knew you'd be there, Daddy."

"I knew you'd be there, Daddy"—faith in its purest form from the lips of a seven-year-old.

Before my open-heart surgery, I was thrown under the boat, drowning in pain and the excess fluid in my lungs. But by the grace of God, I somehow kept saying Lee's faith-filling refrain, "I knew You'd be there, Daddy."

Nurse Jolie, Kelley Brown, the thief on the cross, and countless other believers have found God's fatherly presence and tender, trustworthy affection in simple faith when the boat was capsized and nothing but darkness surrounded them.

The words that "strangely warmed" the desperately searching hearts of Martin Luther in the 1500s and John Wesley in the 1700s will, perhaps, also warm your heart today:

"The righteous man shall live by faith" (Romans 1:17).

Grace alone through faith alone in Christ alone—salvation. A love that will *never* let us go.

13
CHECK YOUR CHAINS

DURING THE 1930S rise of Adolf Hitler and the spread of his iron-willed fascist philosophy, deeply rooted in Darwinist "preservation of favored races" dogma, a society of Aryan German Christians began to bind together and prevail in churches across Germany. This highly bigoted reasoning delighted Hitler and fed his hatred for Germany's Jewish population, singling them out as "impure" elements of the "stronger and more pure" German heritage.

A young dissident named Dietrich Bonhoeffer began to establish a counter movement known as the "Bethel confession," which challenged the New Reich and the scripturally errant German National Church that supported it.

As his disdain for the mistreatment of Germany's Jewish people grew, the young pastor reached the difficult conclusion that killing the Führer was the only way to end his cruel, murderous regime. After two failed attempts to assassinate Hitler, Bonhoeffer was arrested and imprisoned for treason.

During his years of public resistance and his mistreatment in prison, like the apostle Paul whom he deeply admired, Bonhoeffer would influence not only the German church, but also the church of the world through his many writings. Through those writings and the sacrificial lifestyle he practiced with such magnificent, deep conviction, Bonhoeffer would transform the thinking of Jesus-followers for generations to come.

After observing the results of lukewarm Christianity that would corrupt an entire nation and cause the German church to turn its head or even support the practice of Jewish extermination, Bonhoeffer raised the bar for a true Christ-follower to the level Jesus intended. In his book *The Cost of Discipleship*, Bonhoeffer wrote these famous words: "When Jesus calls a person, he bids him to come and die."[1]

The apostle Paul—after his misguided years of leading the persecution of the early church, his miraculous conversion on the road to Damascus, his 17 years of preparation for Christian service, and his heaven-guided missionary journeys across Southern Asia and Europe—wrote this declaration of surrender: "I have been crucified with Christ; and it is no longer I who live, but Christ lives in me" (Galatians 2:20).

Knowing Jesus deeply, a disciple reaches his or her greatest peak of intimacy when he or she receives Him by faith, walks with Him in complete devotion, and dies with Him in complete surrender.

To the mountain climber, the 29,029-foot ascent to the peak of Mount Everest is the supreme trophy of all mountain climbs. To the Christ-follower, the ever-increasing motivation to "die in the flesh" and "walk in the Spirit," knowing that the more you die, the more He lives; the more you sacrifice, the more He rewards; the less you live for yourself, the more fully you give Him the glory—this is the greatest quest of a lifetime. This is the most fulfilling relationship imaginable.

BONDSERVANTS OF JESUS

I was invited, in two successive weeks, to speak to the Jacksonville Jaguars and Green Bay Packers football teams. Coincidentally, both teams were competing against my beloved Dallas Cowboys.

The night before I left for Dallas to be with the Jaguars, I asked God for a vision of what He wanted me to communicate to the two teams. At about 12:30 a.m., He placed a vivid picture in my mind. I felt His urge to go into those two pregame chapels and describe what the apostle Paul meant when he repeatedly identified himself as a "bondservant of Christ."

In the early days of the Christian faith after Jesus' resurrection, His followers endured extensive and horrific persecution under Nero, Domitian, and Marcus Aurelius, supreme leaders of the oppressive Roman government in the first and second centuries. Beginning with the 11 original disciples and spreading throughout early Christendom, followers of Jesus would gladly refer to themselves as "bondservants [Greek *doulos*] of Jesus."

In that day of extensive human slavery, it was generally known that a bondservant was a person who was once a slave but, through the grace of his or her master, had been set free. The former slave, however, loved the master so much that he or she would say, "My love for you is greater than my freedom, greater than my life."

By the thousands, these bondservants of Jesus were paraded into the foreboding Colosseum and Circus Maximus of Rome, where they were slaughtered by gladiators and ravenous wild animals.

In his epic book *Foxe's Book of Martyrs*, John Foxe recounted the inspirational story of the Bishop of Smyrna in the second century, an 86-year-old gentleman named Polycarp.[2] Apprehended by the henchmen of Marcus Aurelius in AD 161, the aging bishop was ushered into the Roman stadium where so many of his contemporaries had suffered and died before him. As a torturous death awaited him, Polycarp was presented before a tribunal and asked to deny Christ. "Consider thyself and have pity on thy own age," he was told.

He was then urged by the proconsul, "Swear, and I will release thee—reproach Christ."

To which Polycarp responded, "Eighty and six years I have served Him, and He never once wronged me; how then shall I blaspheme my King, who hath saved me?"

At this rebuke the proconsul responded, "I will tame thee with fire."

Polycarp, sealing his sentence of death, confidently placed his faith in his Savior and responded, "You threaten me with fire which burns for an hour and is soon extinguished, but the fire of future judgment and of eternal punishment reserved for the ungodly, you are ignorant of. But why do you delay? Do whatever you please."

It was with that same sense of resolve and surrender that I shared with the Jags and Packers the invitation to "give it all" and devoutly follow Christ to the end.

In Green Bay, I gave an invitation to respond with God's call from 2 Chronicles 16:9: "For the eyes of the LORD move to and fro throughout the earth that He may strongly support those whose heart is completely His." In my hand I held a link of chain representing the one man in that pregame chapel who was willing to say, "Jesus, if You would die for me, the least I can do is to live for You. Here is my life."

I had barely finished when Reggie White, an All-Pro defensive edge rusher, walked up to the podium. I shook Reggie's big, inviting hand and looked deeply into his tender, brown eyes. "Reggie," I asked, "how're your chains?"

"Good and tight," he responded. "Good and tight."

Twenty or so other Packers joined Reggie in his response to the invitation.

Hundreds of thousands of links later, in events in various parts of the world, the "Reggies" have come forward to respond to Jesus' love, accept the challenge, and seal their commitment to be His bondservant, leaving their worthless habits and failures at the cross and committing themselves to "give it all" and know Him as Lord and King.

At one college event in Tuscaloosa, Alabama, as hundreds of "Roll Tide" students came to the cross to take the bondservant challenge, a tall, handsome, athletic student led the pack. Through uncontrollable tears, he shared with me the helpless pain he experienced as an addict to pornography. He told me he had a daily habit of viewing illicit sexual material on his computer. As he took the chain link of bondservant surrender from my hand, I saw, in the look on his face, the chains of slavery fall from his wrists.

I took his cell phone number and called him two years later to ask, "Ben, are you still clean?"

Without hesitating, he replied, "Yes, from the night I became a bondservant, I have never gone back into slavery."

Later, Ben wrote me this insightful letter:

Porn controlled me. I was numb. I had lost all my feelings. I hadn't cried for five years. Every night I'd wait 'til everyone was asleep and go to my bedroom for one more hit. Porn controlled me all day long. Everything in my day was built around my porn addiction. It destroyed all my morals. It totally devalued all women. I couldn't have a friendship with a girl. It was all about sex. Porn ruins your life. There's no normalcy. I even put a picture of myself on a website to attract more girls for sex. I look back at that and am so ashamed. It was disgusting. Porn destroyed me as a man, it took away all my manhood. Even though I was in college, I became a child. I'd imagine it. I'd dream about it. I became an addicted liar. Then came the night at the cross. It was a night of delivery. A night of complete transformation. There wasn't enough paper in that huge room for me to write all my sins on. There weren't enough nails to pound all my sins to that cross. But I finally saw the love of God. I saw God's grace. I realized I was forgiven. I said, "Lord, heal me." The Holy Spirit broke all my chains, and like the snap of my fingers it was gone. I knew I was forgiven for all of it. That was two and a half years ago, and I've never gone back. I'm dating an amazing girl now, and I treat her like a queen. I've made a commitment to her that she'll never be touched in a sexual way again until her wedding night. I have guys who hold me accountable to my commitments not to get in compromising places with her. I still get chills and cry when I think about that night at the cross. My life was totally transformed.

A female student from Oklahoma joined the movement and took the challenge. After the event she wrote, "My whole life I have been addicted to my body image. Tonight, after I became a bondservant, I looked into my mirror and for the first time in my life I saw myself in the image of Christ."

One NFL linebacker joined 10,000 men at an event in Michigan. At 225 pounds, he led a pack of 3,000 who responded to the challenge. He wept so profusely I had to hold him upright with a big body-to-body "daddy hug." As we embraced at the foot of the cross, he sobbed these words into my ears, "When I was seven, my daddy abused me. I have hated him ever since."

As this dear, gentle giant took the chain link out of my hands, he yielded the chains of bitterness to the One who died on that cross to "bring liberty to the captives" and tearfully said in resolute faith, "I forgive you, Dad. I forgive you, Dad. I love you, Dad."

There's only room for one chain link on a man's or woman's heart. You can either be chained to some worthless habit, senseless idol, or painful past, or you can be chained to Christ.

I ask you today as I asked Reggie White in Green Bay, Wisconsin, years ago, "How're your chains?"

KNOWING THE HOLY GOD

To FULLY APPRECIATE God's irresistible love for us, we need to understand His holiness. But describing it is difficult. Actually, it's far beyond difficult; it's impossible.

I thought about comparing it to the contaminate-free, pure spring water from the seemingly bottomless Blue Spring on the Current River in southeast Missouri. Nice try, but it's far from perfection. My mind raced back to one unforgettable, majestic evening atop Pedregal Mountain on the southern tip of the Baja Peninsula. The giant, burning, orange solar ball sank into the Pacific Ocean over my western shoulder. Simultaneously, the giant yellow lunar ball arose "out of the water" of the Sea of Cortez over my eastern shoulder. Majestic? Yes. Holy? Hardly. First glance at the Grand Canyon. Awe and wonder? Yes! But holy? Not a chance.

As a spelunker, an unforgettable pristine moment was crawling into a newly opened underground crystal passageway and observing stalactites, stalagmites, and flowstone that no one had ever before seen or touched. It was breathtaking and unforgettable, but a far cry from holy.

I even traveled back a few years to the first glimpse of my two daughters adorned in pristine white lace as they "floated gracefully" on white rose petals down the sacred wedding aisle. Like a rabid Doberman, I had guarded the front door of our home from any boy who sought to place a blemish on that moment! (Ask one of them sometime what I put the high-school boys through who wanted a date with my daughters!) Admiring your daughter in a wedding gown is about as close to holiness as you can get, but it still falls hopelessly short of the mark.

When he was cast into exile on the island of Patmos, the apostle John, caught up in a divine vision from which he wrote the final book in our Bible, described God's holiness best:

> And the four living creatures, each one of them
> having six wings, are full of eyes around and within;
> and day and night they do not cease to say, "Holy,
> holy, holy, is the LORD God, the Almighty, who
> was and who is and who is to come." And when the
> living creatures give glory and honor and thanks
> to Him who sits on the throne, to Him who lives
> forever and ever, the twenty-four elders will fall
> down before Him who sits on the throne, and will
> worship Him who lives forever and ever, and will
> cast their crowns before the throne, saying, "Worthy
> are You, our Lord and our God, to receive glory
> and honor and power; for You created all things,
> and because of Your will they existed, and were
> created. . . ."

> I looked, and I heard the voice of many angels around the throne and the living creatures and the elders; and the number of them was myriads of myriads, and thousands of thousands, saying with a loud voice, "Worthy is the Lamb that was slain to receive power and riches and wisdom and might and honor and glory and blessing." And every created thing which is in heaven and on the earth and under the earth and on the sea, and all things in them, I heard saying, "To Him who sits on the throne, and to the Lamb, be blessing and honor and glory and dominion forever and ever." And the four living creatures kept saying, "Amen." And the elders fell down and worshiped.
>
> REVELATION 4:8-11; 5:11-14

It was He who spoke, and from His breath a cosmos was born.

It was He who placed the earth in a perfectly designed elliptical orbit and tilted precisely at 23.5 degrees on its axis so that life could exist.

It was He who put one billion perfectly sequenced biochemical linguistic notations on every cell in your body and mind.

And it was He who "so loved the world, that He gave His only begotten Son, that whoever believes in Him shall not perish, but have eternal life" (John 3:16).

"Hear, O Israel! The LORD is our God, the LORD is one! You shall love the LORD your God with all your heart and with all your soul and with all your might. These words, which I am commanding you today, shall be on your heart" (Deuteronomy 6:4-6).

HAVE WE LOST THE AWE?

In our wealthy, fast-paced American culture, with an abundance of food, clothing, jewelry, and entertainment at our fingertips, have we lost the same sense of awe His holiness deserves? Have we forgotten the high value of His majesty?

We never considered ourselves poor growing up. My dad worked his daytime dual assignment as intramural athletics director and student activities director at Texas A&M University. At night, he officiated football and basketball games as often as he could. Mom said he made about $3,000 a year. Long before jeans with holes in the knees were in style, we wore our blue jeans, white T-shirts, and socks until we *wore* holes in them. We lived outdoors with our BB guns in the woods, blazing like soldiers, or we played sports. If school wasn't in session, we played outside from sunup to sundown. When my brothers and I each turned nine years old, we had our first jobs selling concessions at the A&M football games. We made $1.50 for four hours' work, but we could eat all the leftover hotdogs we wanted. I don't remember a game that I didn't eat until I was sick to my stomach.

At the school cafeteria, you could buy a Popsicle for a nickel. I always envied the kids who could afford them. Some days a friend would split his with me. I turned into a bit of a beggar; looking back, I laugh at myself.

As the years progressed, my dad's income did as well, but I wouldn't trade *anything* for those days when I craved a nickel! You could buy a Tootsie Pop for two cents in those days. When I had one in my mouth, I thought I was the richest kid on earth!

Love. Cherish. Value. Prize. Delight in. Stand in reverent awe. Fear. Place on the highest pedestal above every person and every thing. These are the terms and phrases I find for God as I scan the Scriptures.

Is it any wonder that He etched the third of the Ten Commandments in the tablet on Mount Sinai in the presence of Moses: "You shall not take the name of the LORD your God in vain" (Exodus 20:7)?

Is it any wonder that when we parade into movie theaters where His name is tossed around so meaninglessly, and often with such blatant profanity and disrespect, our relationship with Him seems so distant?

"The fear of the LORD is the beginning of wisdom," Proverbs 9:10 so aptly cries out.

Yes, He is Dad, but He's not Daddy-O. Yes, He's a friend, but He's not, "What's up, God? How's it going, Buckaroo?" Yes, He is a gift given, but He's not a vending machine.

To fear God is to stand in absolute awe and show the highest respect for His majesty, His holiness, and His power. Jesus knew His Father well when He said in John 15:19 and 17:14, "You are in the world but not of the world" (paraphrased).

It may be PG-13 or TV-14 in Hollywood, but in Scripture, it is profanity and shows the highest disrespect.

To know God deeply is to hear the words of Scripture and heed their cry:

Who is like You among the gods, O LORD? Who is like You, majestic in holiness, awesome in praises, working wonders?

EXODUS 15:11

For God is the King of all the earth; sing praises with a skillful psalm. God reigns over the nations, God sits on His holy throne.

PSALM 47:7-8

More than the sounds of many waters, than the mighty breakers of the sea, the LORD on high is mighty. Your testimonies are fully confirmed; holiness befits Your house, O LORD, forevermore.

PSALM 93:4-5

As you fear and respect our holy God, you will partake in the greatest Father-son, Father-daughter relationship imaginable and actually live in the humbling gratitude of Zephaniah 3:17: "The LORD your God is in your midst, a victorious warrior. He will exult over you with joy, He will be quiet in His love, He will rejoice over you with shouts of joy."

Could anything be more fulfilling and thrilling than that?

LIVING IN REVERENCE

Let me tell you an amazing story of Maximilian Kolbe, a man who understood and lived in the awe and reverence of God's incredible love.

The story takes place in the Nazi prison camp of Auschwitz, the extermination facility for hundreds of thousands of Jews and the Polish sympathizers who hid them from Hitler's heartless killing squads. Kolbe had served as a Franciscan monk and priest for 31 years when he organized a shelter for 2,000 Jewish refugees who had fled Germany. When the shelter was discovered, Kolbe was sentenced to the prison camp.

To intimidate those who would contemplate escape, the

Nazi guards threatened that for each person who tried, 10 cellmates would be thrown into the death bunker until complete starvation claimed their lives.

On August 1, 1941, a prisoner went missing and was assumed to have escaped. The camp deputy commander Karl Fritsch told the prisoners in the missing man's block that 10 others would be locked into the starvation bunker.

One by one, the names were called. When the name of Fran Gajowniczek was announced, he cried in anguish, "My wife! My children!"[1]

Kolbe heroically stepped forward and said, "I am a Catholic priest from Poland. I would like to take his place, because he has a wife and children."[2]

To Gajowniczek's astonishment, the guard granted Kolbe's request. According to an eyewitness, Kolbe led the death bunker prisoners in prayer, constantly standing or kneeling in the middle of the cell. One by one, everyone died except for Kolbe. Finally, wanting to clear the bunker, the guards gave the priest a lethal injection.

After Allied forces overthrew the Nazi regime, the grateful Gajowniczek was reunited with his wife, and he spent his last 50 years telling the story of the sacrificial love of the humble monk who had offered his life as a ransom, an act of kindness that could never be repaid.

In John 15:13, John says, "Greater love has no one than this, that one lay down his life for his friends."

The journey to the heart of Jesus can be costly. But each step of the way, as well as the journey's end, will be wrapped, enveloped, and held fast in His irresistible love.

A CLOSING WORD

In the pages of this book, I've shared my journey to the heart of Jesus. My hope is that it will inspire you and help you in very practical ways to make your own journey. But maybe, like a lot of people I meet these days, you have questions, even doubts. Maybe you wonder, Is everything the Bible says about Jesus' life, death, and resurrection reliable? Is the Bible itself a true account of God and how He has acted in history to create and then redeem us?

I want your journey to be based on a rock-solid faith, not just a vague and shaky hope that the Scriptures and their record of Jesus are true. So I've prepared several documents for your review and consideration, and you'll find them at faithexpedition.com. Here's what you'll discover there:

- Is the Historical Evidence of the Resurrection of Jesus Reliable?
- Is the Scientific Evidence of Creation and Intelligent Design Congruent with Scripture?

- How Do You Know the Bible Is the Word of God?
- How Do You Know Jesus Is Authentic and Historic?

Please take a look, as I believe those materials can help to strengthen your faith. Feel free to pass on that web address to your family and friends as well.

Salvation alone through faith alone in Christ alone—you can stake your eternal destiny on that truth in complete confidence that it's the most real thing in the universe.

APPENDIX

As unto Him

Jesus said in Matthew 25:31-46:

> But when the Son of Man comes in His glory, and
> all the angels with Him, then He will sit on His
> glorious throne. And all the nations will be gathered
> before Him; and He will separate them from one
> another, as the shepherd separates the sheep from the
> goats; and He will put the sheep on His right, and
> the goats on the left.
>   Then the King will say to those on His right,
> "Come, you who are blessed of My Father, inherit
> the kingdom prepared for you from the foundation
> of the world. For I was hungry, and you gave Me
> something to eat; I was thirsty, and you gave me
> something to drink; I was a stranger, and you
> invited Me in; naked, and you clothed Me; I was
> sick, and you visited Me; I was in prison, and you
> came to Me." Then the righteous will answer Him,
> "Lord, when did we see You hungry, and feed You,
> or thirsty, and give You something to drink? And
> when did we see You a stranger, and invite You in, or

naked, and clothe You? When did we see You sick, or in prison, and come to You?" The King will answer and say to them, "Truly I say to you, to the extent that you did it to one of these brothers of Mine, even the least of them, you did it to Me."

Then He will also say to those on His left, "Depart from Me, accursed ones, into the eternal fire which has been prepared for the devil and his angels; for I was hungry, and you gave Me nothing to eat; I was thirsty, and you gave Me nothing to drink; I was a stranger, and you did not invite Me in; naked, and you did not clothe Me; sick, and in prison, and you did not visit Me." Then they themselves also will answer, "Lord, when did we see You hungry, or thirsty, or a stranger, or naked, or sick, or in prison, and did not take care of You?" Then He will answer them, "Truly I say to you, to the extent that you did not do it to one of the least of these, you did not do it to Me." These will go away into eternal punishment, but the righteous into eternal life.

If you would like to serve and please Jesus by helping "the least of these" in our day, I encourage you to contact Cross International, whose motto is "Caring for the World's Poorest of the Poor." You'll find them at crossinternational.org.

NOTES

INTRODUCTION

1. William J. Federer, *America's God and Country Encyclopedia of Quotations* (St. Louis, MO: Amerisearch, 1994), 557.
2. Ibid., 206.
3. "John Grisham: Accepting Jesus Christ Was 'the Most Important Event in My Life,'" *BCNN1 WP*, January 2012.
4. Federer, 31.
5. Ibid., 388.
6. Ibid.
7. "150 Mother Teresa Quotes with Pictures," *Very Best Quotes*, April 25, 2016.
8. Mark Ellis, "LeBron James: Everything Will Be Alright When Jesus Christ Returns," *Charisma News*, December 16, 2015.

CHAPTER 3: HIS LOVE TRANSFORMS

1. John Newton, "Amazing Grace," 1779.
2. *Oxford English Dictionry*, s.v. "grace.

CHAPTER 5: AN AMAZING GOD

1. Christianity.about.com. Christianity Statistics.

CHAPTER 6: GOD'S MESSAGE FOR YOU

1. Robert Jastrow, *Intellectuals Speak Out About God* (New York: Regnery Gateway, 1984).
2. Andrei Linde, "The Self-Reproducing Inflationary Universe," *Scientific American* 271, no. 5 (1994): 48–55.
3. *Chicago Daily News*, April 12, 1936.
4. *Merriam-Webster*, s.v. "cosmos," https://www.merriam-webster.com/dictionary/cosmos.

5. Charles Darwin and Francis Darwin, *The Autobiography of Charles Darwin and Selected Letters* (New York: Dover, 1969), 85.
6. Charles Darwin, *On the Origin of Species by Means of Natural Selection* (Erres e Esses Lda, Portugal,1936).
7. William Shakespeare, Allan Park Paton, Henry Reeve, and Great Britain, *The Hamnet Shakspere: According to the First Folio (spelling Modernised)* Edinburgh: Edmonston, 1879.
8. Fred Hoyle, *The Big Bang in Astronomy, New Scientist* 92, no. 1280 (November 19, 1981), 527.
9. "A Non-Genetic Look at Evolution"; *American Scientists* 41, no. 1 (January 1953), 100, 103.
10. Pierre-Paul Grassé, *Evolution of Living Organisms* (New York: Academic Press, 1977), 88.
11. Dr. Soren Lovtrup, *Darwinism: Refutation of a Myth* (New York: Springer, 1987), 30.
12. Colin Patterson, "*Cladistics*," Interview with Brian Leek, Peter Franz, BBC, March 4, 1982.
13. Darwin, 281–82.
14. Luther D. Sunderland, *Darwin's Enigma: Fossils and Other Problems*, 4th Edition (Green Forest, AK: Master Books, 1998), 89.

CHAPTER 7: MOVING CLOSER TO GOD

1. Earl Nightingale, *The Strangest Secret*, 1956 (Spoken word record).
2. "Healthy Lifestyle: Adult Health," Mayo Clinic. April 14, 2016.

CHAPTER 9: KNOWING GOD THROUGH TRIALS

1. John of the Cross, "The Dark Night," *The Collected Works of St. John of the Cross*. Trans. Kieran Kavanaugh and Otilio Rodriguez (Washington, DC: ICS Publications, 1991), 50–52.
2. John of the Cross, "The Spiritual Canticle Stanza 9–11," *The Collected Works of St. John of the Cross*. Trans. Kieran Kavanaugh and Otilio Rodriguez. (Washington, DC: ICS Publications, 1991), 472–473.

CHAPTER 10: KNOWING GOD BY MAKING DISCIPLES

1. *The State of Discipleship: A Barna Report Produced in Partnership with The Navigators* (Colorado Springs: NavPress, 2015).
2. Dallas Willard, *The Great Omission: Reclaiming Jesus's Essential Teachings on Discipleship* (San Francisco: HarperSanFrancisco, 2006).
3. Ibid.
4. Ibid.
5. Ibid.
6. John S. Dickerson, *The Great Evangelical Recession: 6 Factors That Will*

Crash the American Church . . . and How to Prepare (Grand Rapids, MI: Baker, 2013).

CHAPTER 11: HELP FROM THE HOLY SPIRIT
1. Robert Munger, *My Heart—Christ's Home* (Downer's Grove, IL: IVP Books, 1986).

CHAPTER 13: CHECK YOUR CHAINS
1. Dietrich Bonhoeffer, *The Cost of Discipleship* (New York: Macmillan, 1959), 99.
2. John Foxe and G. A. Williamson, *Foxe's Book of Martyrs* (Boston: Little, Brown, 1966).

CHAPTER 14: KNOWING THE HOLY GOD
1. St. Maximilian Kolbe, Catholicpages.com, accessed June 24, 2019, http://www.catholic-pages.com/saints/st_maximilian.asp.
2. Maximillan Kolbe, Jewish Virtual Library, accessed June 24, 2019, https://www.jewishvirtuallibrary.org/maximilian-kolbe.

ABOUT THE AUTHOR

JOE WHITE and his wife, Debbie-Jo, run a family of Christian sports camps that attract 23,000 children each summer from around the world. Joe has written more than 20 books and speaks to men's, women's, and students' conferences, to NFL teams, and on Christian radio.

He played nose tackle for the SMU Mustangs and coached the defensive line at Texas A&M. He has been awarded two honorary doctoral degrees and was named one of the "Top Ten Influencers of the Century" by *New Man* magazine.

Joe and Debbie-Jo have been married more than 44 years at the time of this writing and have been blessed with four children and 13 grandchildren.